Write Well & Sell:

Changing Life's Simple Stories Into Sales

exclamation points
cf. Lamott ↑xIV

The Blueprint Series
Guides for Practical Writing

Write Well & Sell:

Changing Life's Simple Stories Into Sales

by
Judith Burnett Schneider

Jam-Packed Press
Pittsburgh, PA

ISBN 1-892356-02-3

Dedication

To Mom and Dad,
who have forever encouraged me to be all that I
am.

To Timmy,
whose faith in me has always been greater than my
dreams.

To Jacqueline, Juliana and Timothy,
who are the reasons for my exhaustion and my
exhilaration!

Acknowledgments

I am indebted to Mary Jo Rulnick and Sandra Louden for their friendship and dedication. We did it!

I wish to acknowledge my nieces, Jill, Kassie, Megan, and Stephanie Burnett who spent precious hours with my children while I wrote and edited, edited and rewrote.

I, also, wish to acknowledge Brigitte McDonald and Bob Brayton, for their patience while listening to my "creative" ideas.

I am sincerely grateful to Robin Stahl who carries the esteemed title, My First Editor. Thank you for having the courage to publish an unknown writer's work.

I thank my long-time friend, Cheryl Smith, who gave me my first copy of Writer's Market so many years ago.

I wish to acknowledge Dr. Harry Krebs, Professor of Asian Philosophy at Dickinson College, for recognizing and encouraging a "competence", long before I decided to utilize it.

Contents

CRAVING THE CAFFEINE
LONGING TO WRITE

I sat alone at a locally held writer's conference and scanned the room. I had just had my second child and spent the past two years absorbed in diapers and doused with strained carrots. And, contrary to what you might think, I felt completely fulfilled.

But my mom—the mother of seven—knew it would be healthy for me to get out and pursue some mental stimulation, whether it led to anything or not. It was she who convinced me to go to the writer's conference that day—that transitional day when my writing life changed from journal entries to potential sales, from experimental dabbling to laying the groundwork for a lifelong career.

As I scanned the room, I spotted an older woman, much older—possibly in her late eighties—taking notes.

"That'll be me," I thought. "If I don't try to sell my writing now, I'll be 90 and wishing I had."

Without my realizing it, the elderly woman became my motivation.

Where to begin? How could I make the transition from self-satisfying journal writing to something that would please others—something with potential to sell?

I started with the local library. I read every how-to book in the writing section. Some of them, I read twice. I learned how to write novels, short stories, magazine articles, romance, poetry, mysteries, children's stories, and even creative non-fiction.

After much thought and groundwork, I decided to write about what I was closest to at the time—about what would require little research, because getting to the library with a newborn and a toddler would be difficult, I was certain.

I wrote about myself.

Since that motivational experience—observing the older woman—I have become dedicated, committed, *addicted* to my writing. I enjoy it, need it, and am not the same without my daily dose.

There is another thing I've grown addicted to in recent years—**coffee**. In fact, I'm always in search of the perfect cup, much like I strive for perfection in my essay writing. Both are tempting at the start, fulfilling in the middle and satisfying even after they're gone.

Through this book, I have but one goal—to save you time. By following my suggestions for testing your ideas, enhancing your writing and editing your work, you will write memorable essays—recognizable for both uniqueness and clarity. After reading this book, your essays will be exceptionally well-written, technically superb and topically sound.

You will move from writing personal journal

entries to selling professional, publishable essays.

I thank you for making the effort to purchase this book, for choosing to propel yourself toward your goal of writing well. I am anxious to share my experiences with you and hope to help you fulfill your creative dreams.

BONUS TIP: As you read this book, keep a notebook nearby. Jot down interesting ideas, clever titles and phrases, and unique situations as they bubble up from your subconscious or present themselves in your everyday life.

BONUS TIP: A writer's subconscious works overtime—in traffic, at work, even in dreams. **Always be sure to have** *quill and scroll* **on hand**—in the car, in your pocket and especially on that nearby nightstand. I like to keep a notebook and pencil near the television, too. You never know when a topic of interest will appear on a news show. Get in the habit of sending for transcripts. They cost a few dollars each and usually contain current information that is not readily available elsewhere.

NOTE: Throughout this book, I will refer to your life's simple stories as "personal essays" for simplicity and clarity.

Chapter One

COFFEE CATEGORIZING
ESSAY CLASSIFICATION

Personal essays either highlight an event in the author's life—including particular effects on the author—or reveal the author's sentiments concerning a specific subject or current event and why. Essays are either emotive, reflective, or both.

In general, **most essays evoke some sort of emotion. That's the point.** Some actually draw the reader through a *range* of feelings, from empathy to elation. This type of essay, in my opinion, is the most enjoyable to experience *and* the most difficult to write.

For simplicity and ease of reference, I have divided the types of personal essays into the following categories.

EMOTIONAL

The author tells of a happening which directly affected her* in either a positive or a negative light. While reading the emotional essay, the reader generally reacts by empathizing with the author.

---

* When referring to writers, readers and editors throughout the text, I will use forms of *she* and *he* interchangeably.

Example:
I wrote an essay about my husband and I weathering a snowstorm to reach a romantic sleigh ride destination. This essay, called "The Saint Valentine's Day Sleighing", evokes positive emotion.

HUMOROUS
The author tells a light-hearted account of some event or personal experience. This type of essay pokes fun at the event or at some aspect of the author's personality. The intention of the humorous essay is primarily to entertain the reader.
Example:
My essay, called "Masked Revenge", is a humorous account of the Halloween night when I tricked my husband by sneaking into the basement, putting on a gorilla costume, prowling around the outside of the house and ringing the front door bell.

INTROSPECTIVE
The author examines her own thoughts and feelings and extrapolates from them. Often, the author's intention is to leave the reader with some kind of thought-stimulating message.
Example:
I wrote an essay, entitled "holocaust", about a visit to the United States Holocaust Memorial Museum in Washington, D.C. and its effect on me.

INSPIRATIONAL
The author tells an account of an emotionally

moving occurrence or revelation that changed his outlook on life. By comprehending the inspirational essay, the reader might have a related emotional response which affects him, even if only temporarily.

Example:

One essay I wrote, entitled "Second Election, First Lesson", highlights a pivotal point in my life when, in sixth grade, I learned the difficult lesson that life isn't always fair.

Personal essays are not always so distinctively defined. One essay could cross the boundaries of the above classifications. Some of my most serious, introspective pieces have humor woven in. Often, it provides a necessary release of tension. Let your imagination run free to enhance your thoughts and expand your ideas.

NOTE: What about opinion pieces? I am frequently asked why I have not included opinion pieces in my essay classifications. Opinion writing *is* personal in that the author gives her sentiments on a current topic of interest. She does not, however, always tell how the outcome of this topic has affected or changed her life—primarily because it usually hasn't. It is merely opinion, *not* personal experience.

While it is true personal essays offer opinion, they actually contain much, much more.

In order to determine which type of essay you are most likely to write—at least, at first—take the following quiz.

COFFEE CATEGORIZING QUIZ
WHAT TYPE OF ESSAYIST ARE YOU?

Do you pack your stories with sweet adjectives and creamy metaphors? Do you prefer a sprinkle of light-heartedness over downright bitter humor? Do you burn your mouth on your openings, then end with a pleasing aftertaste? Read and answer the following questions to find out what type of essayist you are or can be.

1. When you accidentally lock your keys in the car, the first thing you do is...
    a. flag down a passer-by and ask for help.
    b. try to break in through the car window or door.
    c. thank your lucky stars the car wasn't running and your child wasn't in the car seat.
    d. stand stunned and ask yourself, "How could I have done something so stupid?"
    e. find a phone.

2. When you have a full cart of groceries and the man behind you has one loaf of bread, you...
    a. ask him if he would like to check out ahead of you.
    b. only allow him go ahead of you if he asks.
    c. do nothing and wonder whether he thinks you're rude for not allowing him to check out before you.
    d. make him wait, then feel satisfied you held your ground. You would never jump ahead of anyone else and he shouldn't either.
    e. strike up a conversation with him about how embarrassed you are that your cart is full.

3. If you are stuck in stop-dead traffic, you...
    a. read the novel on the seat next to you.
    b. get out of your car to find out what's going on.
    c. pick up your car phone and call a friend.
    d. hope it isn't an accident causing the traffic jam.
    e. remind yourself to pull off and have your oil changed.

4. A friend calls and asks you to come over right away. She needs to consult with you on how to handle a temperamental neighbor. You don't have the time, so you...
   a. tell her you're busy and you'll call her tomorrow.
   b. weigh how much the friend means to you, then decide.
   c. drop everything and go. Life is too short to let this moment of need pass.
   d. tell her you must finish what you're doing, but you'll be over in an hour.
   e. say, "Look, you don't need that pain-in-the-neck neighbor anyway."

5. When looking through sweaters hanging on a rack in a department store, one falls. You...
   a. leave it on floor and move to another area.
   b. pick it up, even though no one saw you, and put it back on the hanger.
   c. pick up the sweater and toss it over the top of the rack, without a hanger. Hey, you did more than most people would.
   d. hang it up, only if someone saw you drop it.
   e. kick it under the rack. The night janitor will be glad you gave him something to do.

6. You're talking to an acquaintance and see he has a crumb on his face. You...
   a. brush your face with your hand, hoping he'll brush his.
   b. brush it off of him yourself. You hate to see anyone looking vulnerable.
   c. tell him. You would want him to do the same for you.
   d. don't call it to his attention, but can't seem to keep from staring at the thing.
   e. laugh at him for having the crumb hanging there, confident he'll laugh with you.

7. When the electricity goes out for an extended period of time, you...
   a. go to a hotel.
   b. go to a relative's or friend's house.
   c. call the local news channel and enjoy making a big deal.
   d. rent a generator, but find it emits toxic fumes.
   e. light a candle and stick it out.

ANSWER SHEET
WHAT TYPE OF ESSAYIST ARE YOU?

Circle your answers below, then transfer the image shown next to your answer to the blank on the right. Tally up the images and, in the **OVERALL** blank, record the one that appears the most. Then, read about what type of essayist you are or will be.

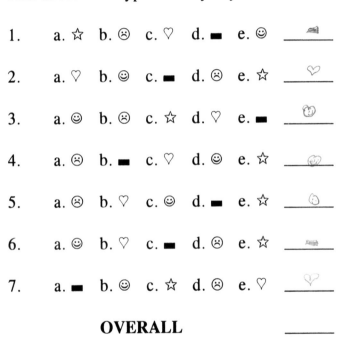

1.   a. ☆   b. ☹   c. ♡   d. ▬   e. ☺   ____

2.   a. ♡   b. ☺   c. ▬   d. ☹   e. ☆   ____

3.   a. ☺   b. ☹   c. ☆   d. ♡   e. ▬   ____

4.   a. ☹   b. ▬   c. ♡   d. ☺   e. ☆   ____

5.   a. ☹   b. ♡   c. ☺   d. ▬   e. ☆   ____

6.   a. ☺   b. ♡   c. ▬   d. ☹   e. ☆   ____

7.   a. ▬   b. ☺   c. ☆   d. ☹   e. ♡   ____

OVERALL   ____

SCORING
WHAT TYPE OF ESSAYIST ARE YOU?

If one image dominates your answer sheet, you're lucky. Your ideas can be easily categorized. If your results are tied, congratulations. You're a combination and you're unique.

☺ CAPPUCCINO—POSITIVE EMOTION

You love to tell a good story with a smooth, creamy ending. You see the things that happen to you, mostly in a positive light.

☹ ESPRESSO—NEGATIVE EMOTION

You are a nuts and bolts kind of person. You talk straight and tell it like it is, even if the end result is negative. Sometimes, you even *enjoy* the impact of telling the dismal truth.

☆IRISH COFFEE—HUMOROUS

You get a kick out of people and the happenings around you. You actually enjoy taking a chance at being different. Odd things strike you as funny, even in your own personality. You are completely comfortable poking fun at others and yourself.

■ PLAIN BLACK—INTROSPECTIVE

You tend to internalize, and that's not such a bad thing. You reflect on situations as they arise and determine their ultimate affect on you and your surroundings. No cream and sugar for you.

♡ CAFE MOCHA—INSPIRATIONAL

You see the good in everything and everyone and want to spread the news accordingly. You delight in other's happiness and want to share the wonderful things that have happened to you. Your hint of chocolate reflects a splash of spirituality.

Again, not all essays fit neatly into only one of these categories. In fact, most don't. There is no need to feel bound by the results of this quiz. It merely provides a starting point, a place for you to begin to focus your writing energies.

If you intend to write about a mishap and it turns out to be a humorous story, that's okay. Flexibility is the appeal of the personal essay.

In other words, there is no essay "formula". As long as the story flows and it works, go with it—feel comfortable, enjoy.

Chapter Two

EXPERIENCE THE AROMA
THE ESSENCE OF IDEAS

The first thing that hits you when you seek the perfect cup of coffee is the essence of the aromatic blend.

The first thing that hits the essayist is the *idea.*

But how do writers come up with their ideas?

"My life isn't exciting", new writers tell me. "I have nothing to write about," they say.

In response, I ask them to answer this question:

If an international terrorist came into your living room and forced you to leave with only two of your earthly possessions—one practical and one sentimental—what would you choose?

Before you answer, get down to the bare essentials, for the practical possession, and down to the deeply meaningful for the sentimental. Then, ask yourself why you chose what you did? Write down your answers in your newly-acquired essay notebook.

An alternate challenge would be to come up with something sentimental that is also practical and vice versa.

HINT: In answering the above, you have uncovered the seed of an idea for at least two essays.

The next section further discusses how to obtain ideas, organize them and decide about which idea you should begin to write.

To assist you, I have put together this list of idea guidelines. Following these suggestions will help you to focus on what it is you want to write.

WRITE WHAT YOU WANT TO WRITE

Seasoned writers give the advice, "Write what you know." I disagree. We are saturated with what we "know" and seek asylum from our everyday lives including our jobs, our lifestyles, even our hobbies. This is why, I believe, you must **write what you want to write**. But what does that mean? How do you know what you want to write?

It might be easier to identify what you *don't* want to write. When a friend says, "Wasn't that great when we went rafting down the Colorado River? You should write about that," you think, "I should."

Then, something inside shouts back, "But I don't *want* to write about that."

Writers of magazine articles and textbooks must write what they know or write what *other* people are interested in, but you, as an essayist, do not. You are virtually unrestricted.

So, **don't restrict yourself**. Simply **write what you are compelled to write**, no matter what. Write the story the way you want to write it, the way you remember it. Just choose your topic and write. We'll address the consequences later.

USE YOUR NEGATIVES

Some people have obvious negatives in their lives, like one author I know, Sally Alexander, who is blind. And while she doesn't actually consider her blindness a negative, she does admit she has sold many books for children and adults on topics related to her disability.

How can you discover and use your own negatives? Tap into the feeling you experienced when you were most alone, vulnerable. Remember the rage you felt when you were misjudged or treated unfairly. Re-live the hurt you experienced when you were last betrayed. What frightens you, disturbs you, saddens you?

You might be reluctant to draw upon these negative events and wonder why I am asking you to do so. Unfortunately, or fortunately, **negativity sells**. I once read about a study which stated, and I paraphrase, when someone has a good experience, she tells an average of **four** people. The same study showed when the average person has a bad or negative experience, she tells **sixty** people about the incident.

I repeat, *negativity sells*.

PROVOKE BUT DON'T OFFEND

You want to stimulate those who read your essays but not offend them. If your topic is extremely controversial or weighted heavy with opinion, you can still write the piece, but your market choices and chances for sale will be narrowed considerably.

BE CERTAIN YOU'RE COMFORTABLE WITH THE SUBJECT

Ask yourself, "Can I talk openly about this topic? Is this something I *want* to write about?"

Example:

I wrote an essay, called "The Magic of the Little Blue Cookbook", about how my husband preferred my cooking when I used a cookbook compiled by his mother. I liked the essay but didn't realize—until I read it aloud to my critique group—I was holding back. There was restriction or retention between the lines. Upon their calling this to my attention, I was able to admit I felt guilty writing about my husband's mother when I had never written about my own.

This inner uneasiness about which I wasn't consciously aware interfered with the flow of the essay. I have never sent it out for publication.

THINK UNIQUE

You decide you are an ordinary person leading an ordinary life. And while you're satisfied with your happy upbringing and are a fairly well-adjusted adult, you ask, "What can I write about?"

Every bride cherishes her wedding day and each mother holds dear the moment her child was born. But these events are common, not unique. Lots of people have similar experiences. So, oddly enough, I encourage you **not** to write about those ordinary special occasions in your life.

Think beyond the norm, past those special events many people experience. Focus on your everyday life. What do you take for granted? What do you do, as a matter of routine, that other people find fascinating? Is there some unusual happening in your past which would interest readers? Have you ever encountered a famous person?

✓ Celebrity Connections

Believe it or not, I once stayed overnight at comedian Rosie O'Donnell's house—I could tell you the name of her late dog and the nickname only her old friends call her.

Another time, I asked Rocky Bleier, professional football star and motivational speaker, which of his four superbowl rings was his favorite. He told me, then allowed me to try it on. It was as heavy as an ingot and nearly large enough to fit as a bracelet.

To top it all, I've received writing advice from super-author and syndicated columnist, Dave Barry.

No matter how brief, positive moments like these—when written into an essay—can really grab an editor's attention. Face it, everybody loves a celebrity story. But no negative reflections, please. Leave that to the tabloid writers.

INTROSPECTIVE QUIZ
WHAT MAKES ME UNIQUE?

To uncover the essence of your individuality, you must indulge in self-examination. The following questions are introspective, personal, revealing, and often difficult to answer. Take the time to think before you answer. Be as specific as possible. Record all thoughts in your nearby notebook.

1. Who seems to take an interest in you? Don't think about who you gravitate toward, but who do you continually bump into? Who always seems to be there for you?

2. When do people ask your advice? When do you feel good about having helped someone? In what capacity do you come to their aid?

3. To what do people respond when you engage in conversation? About what do they want to hear more? What, about you, interests others?

4. Where do you stand out? When do you hear, "You're really good at that" or "That's what I like about you"?

5. Why do you react the way you do? What makes you envious? What makes you smile? When are you afraid?

6. Do you know your strengths and weaknesses? What are your good habits and bad? What personality trait would you like to change?

7. How do people describe you? Think about the simple things. Are you a reader, a coffee drinker, a nail-biter? Are you dependent and needy or self-sufficient and strong?

In answering these questions honestly, you are becoming comfortable with what makes you different. This comfort level is important to achieve *before* you begin to write.

IDEA EXERCISE

Complete the following as quickly and thoroughly as possible. Don't worry if you haven't written the best answer. **Write whatever comes to mind,** but if you arrive at a one-word answer, please elaborate. Expand on your ideas as much as you can in the limited time allowed.

For the first time through, give yourself 30 seconds, maximum, to complete each phrase in your notebook.

1. Boy, was I fuming when...

2. If I have to say so myself, I'm darn good at...

3. I was completely embarrassed when...

4. I cried when...

5. I wonder why...

6. I couldn't believe it when I heard...

7. I'll admit I felt jealous when...

8. I still can't believe I ever...

9. I was absolutely petrified when...

10. A happy childhood memory was...

11. One trick I always use is...

12. I laughed myself to tears when...

13. I felt the most unselfish when I...

14. The one thing I'll never do again is...

15. I had a heavy, heavy heart the day I...

Take a few minutes to expand on your answer to number 15. It might be difficult, but attempt to recall your feelings and the effects they had on you and others. Try to remember details of the events leading up to that moment and the repercussions that played themselves out, afterward.

In doing so, you are developing, expanding, fleshing out your essay idea.

Go back through the above exercise and, this time, don't limit your time. Notice how your answers change as you have more time to ponder each phrase.

In taking this quiz twice, with and without a time constraint, you have come up with as many as 30 ideas—all with the potential to become completed essays.

BONUS TIP: Take the quiz in a few months and note how your answers change, again. These additional answers offer even more potential essay ideas.

IDEA EXERCISE AFTERTHOUGHTS

These questions were designed to evoke emotion and to zero in on your own unique experiences. These are the stories that sell—the interesting and the unusual.

But you ask, "How can any of these simple sentences become full essays?"

Take the following as an example. I once asked myself to recall my most embarrassing moment. I wrote this on an index card:

I often think about the time I dressed up a day early for Halloween. For some reason, that moment still embarrasses me.

These two sentences became the basis for "The Ears of Halloween", an essay I wrote which sold locally to *The Pittsburgh Tribune-Review*, then to the 10th largest newspaper in the country, *The Cleveland Plain Dealer*. The story invariably sparks interest and stirs curiosity in every class, workshop or conference lecture I deliver. A condensed version of the complete essay can be found in Appendix A.

In addition, I am in the process of writing a children's picture book about a girl who dresses up on the wrong day.

All this from one simple thought jotted on an index card.

BONUS TIP: Don't begin your essay using the exact phrases in The Idea Exercise. While they make great idea inducers, they are **not** good opening lines. We'll discuss strong openings in Chapter Five.

KEEP AN IDEA FILE

You might have begun reading this book with one or two ideas, but I would like you to close with

30, maybe more. With this many ideas, though, how can you keep them organized?

The most important thing is to **write down your ideas** and to **keep them in one place**. Don't rely on memory.

I collect ideas in an inexpensive index card file box. You can use an envelope, a drawer, a file folder, whatever. You don't even have to alphabetize or categorize them, although I do. Just keep them all together, so you know where to look when you want to spark your creativity.

Chapter Three

ALLOW FOR BREWING TIME
TEST THE IDEA

Now that you have a file full of ideas, how do you know if any of your sketchy notions will make a good essay?

Answer the following questions relative to your individual ideas to test if each is strong enough to support a complete essay and sell.

IDEA TEST
CAN YOUR IDEA SURVIVE?

1. **WHO** will be interested in this story? Who is the target audience?

2. **WHEN** should it be published? Can it be tied to a certain holiday, season, or upcoming event? [If so, you must submit 6-8 weeks ahead of time for newspapers, and six months or more in advance for magazines.]

3. **WHERE** could it be published? Have I seen this type of essay before? If so, where?

4. **WHY** is the story significant?

5. **HOW** is it different?

6. **WILL** the story offend anyone? If so, who and why?

7. **DOES** the story have enough depth to hold the reader's interest for 600-1200 words?

8. **HAVE** all the repercussions been played out? Is this event completely over? [It is more difficult to write about a current situation than it is a past experience.]

9. **DOES** the story have a beginning that will capture the interest of the reader?

10. **WHAT** is my theme, my thread, holding the story together?

11. **WILL** the essay come to a satisfying conclusion?

12. **IS** my essay idea believable and can it be told in a logical order?

After you have answered these general questions about your essay idea, it is time to focus on the specifics of the story.

COLLECT RANDOM THOUGHTS & ORDER THEM

How do you know which idea will lead to a salable essay? Which idea should you work on?

Examine your answers from the Idea Quiz in Chapter Two. Pick the one that most stimulates your feelings. Think about that idea for a few days, as often as possible—in the shower, on your way to the grocery store, in the doctor's office. Jot down facts, thoughts and phrases, relevant or not, as they come to you and keep them in your notebook, envelope or file.

Don't worry about word choice or sentence structure. Simply write what comes to mind. You'll be surprised, after a week's time, how many thoughts you have accumulated.

If your jottings are few in number, move on to a new idea. Answer another question and start again.

Once you have collected enough ideas in your envelope, perform the following Order Test.

THE ORDER TEST

If you find you have a collection of notes in your notebook or envelope for one particular idea, you will need to put the points in order to see if they form a logical, readable, writable essay.

In order to *order*, ask the following questions:

1. Which point is the most "personally" emphatic? Which **strikes you**, really hits home? Try this as your opening, serving to captivate or intrigue the reader.

2. Which point **tells the problem** or describes the uniqueness of the situation? This could be used immediately after the opening in order to inform the reader of your intention. It will let the reader know, in which direction you are heading.

3. Do any combinations of the jottings seem to reveal a **pattern or sequence**? These may be arranged in succession of increasing importance or tension, making up the middle of your story.

4. Do any points have **flair, zip, zing**? Use these as a the story's climax.

5. Does any one point seem to **summarize the issue**? Place this, just after the climax and before the ending. This point can serve to link the climax to the closing.

6. Which point is most **thought-provoking**? This one might make a strong, memorable ending.

7. File supporting **leftover points** in the proper categories above. This will help to flesh out the story.

THE ENVELOPE EXERCISE

Still unsure how to perform The Order Test on your own idea? Try this Envelope Exercise on one of mine.

The following list consists of 13 separate points related to my Florida vacation, cut short by an approaching hurricane. I remembered these points randomly and collected them in an envelope.

Read each point and ask yourself the questions contained in **The Order Test** on the previous page. You might want to copy the points on index cards, for ease of shuffling.   Put each statement in the appropriate category. If a particular point fits in more than one category, jot it down twice.

Remember, you can't get the order wrong. Ordering the points differently will simply result in a different essay.

The Envelope Contents:

A. After hearing of the approaching hurricane, my husband, my baby and I went out to dinner. I couldn't eat.

B. We went to the grocery store to buy formula for the baby. An eery silence fell over the shoppers. People solemnly checked-out with cans of tuna and bottled water. Many shelves were completely empty.

C. Caravans of people headed north on I-95, away from the hurricane's targeted area.

D. Once home after the vacation, I watched the news with an odd feeling in my stomach.

E.   We caught our flight home within an hour of authorities closing the airport.

F. Afterward, I read accounts of people boarding up windows and surviving in bath tubs.

G. The hurricane was approximately 12 hours away. Our flight home was due to take off in 15 hours.

H. We packed our clothes in silence. We had never left a vacation with such a feeling of despair.

I. My baby was only 18 months old. It was the first time I was responsible for someone else in a *real* crisis.

J. We decided, if the airport were closed, we would continue driving north in the rental car—as far as we could, for as long as the baby would last.

K. I was afraid to be in a 16th floor condominium in 80 mile per hour winds.

L. I had never wanted to be home so badly.

M. We attempted to change our flight to an earlier departure and couldn't. All flights were booked. We were afraid we wouldn't make it out before the hurricane hit.

BONUS TIP: Take note of how some of the points are factual and some emotional. When you are collecting your own random thoughts, write *everything* down, relevant or not. You never know what you will need to complete the essay and strengthen the story.

ENVELOPE EXERCISE ANSWER KEY

There are several ways the contents of this envelope could be ordered. The following is just one example:

1. **Opening**:   point B.
2. **States Problem**:   point G.

3. **Sequential Points/Middle**:   points M, J, and C; points D and F.
4. **Climax**:   point E.
5. **Summary Link**:   point L.
6. **Ending**:   point I.
7. **Leftovers**:   points A, H, and K.

NOTE: You might have chosen L for the opening and E for the ending—or some other combination of points—which will result in a different version of the story. That is the beauty of the personal essay. **Even given the same points, essays are individual—they are distinctive—characteristic of you, the writer.**

BONUS TIP: Using The Envelope Exercise/Order Test is the vehicle through which you will move your personal experience from idea to essay. It enables you to organize your thoughts and prepare, providing the outline or backbone of your story, thus, allowing you to write a better first draft.

Chapter Four

POUR YOURSELF A CUP
WRITE

Now that you've pondered your idea and read about the craft of writing, follow these simple steps to get your story down on paper.

WRITE THE STORY AS IT REALLY HAPPENED

Once you've thought about your essay idea and jotted down key points and catchy phrases, you are ready to write.

The best way to get started is to settle down with your favorite notebook and pen or flip on the computer, clear your mind, and write. Focus, not on style or technique, but on telling the story. Don't worry about the opening line, the sentence structure or word choice. Just get the story on paper. Tell it from beginning to end, including whatever you deem important at the time.

✓ **Write using the first-person format.**
   Example:
Write, "I opened the door to find the stranger facing me." This brings the reader closer to the story

than the third person account, "The suburbanite unlocked the front door, allowing the intruder to enter." This sounds like a news story.

✓ **Write in either the present tense or the simple past.** Writing in the present tense lends an *immediate* feel to your piece but can be difficult to do well. It might be easiest to begin using the simple past tense.

DON'T STOP

Don't leaf through the Thesaurus in search of a more meaningful term or call a friend to check facts. Just write. If you have to correct the spelling of a word or the name of the restaurant, do what I do. Mark your copy and move on.

Example:

"Out of breath, I collapsed **[TH]** on the sidewalk in front of Joe's Cafe **[CHECK]**. The bump on my forehead thumped in rhythm with _____ **???**"

[TH] = THESAURUS. This alerts me to find a synonym for a particular word. I wanted something more descriptive than "collapsed" but couldn't think of it on the spot. In order not to interrupt my thoughts, I simply marked it in brackets and continued to write.

[CHECK] is more universal for me. It might mean I have to check a fact in the encyclopedia, on a map or with a family member who was present at the time. Instead of disrupting the flow of my writing by stopping to make a call or use the dictionary, I use this bracketed message which will jump out at me later, while I'm editing the story.

_____ and/or **???** tells me I couldn't find what I wanted to say at the time. Since I liked the beginning of the sentence, I left it to be completed at another time. If not, I can always delete.

You may use these editorial indications or create your own.

SET REALISTIC GOALS

Don't be surprised if you can't write your entire story in one sitting. Writing, especially personal essays, is mentally and physically draining because you are playing through emotions and struggling to get the facts straight, most of the time going from memory. If you can't seem to keep up the writing pace, take a break for an hour or even a day. But don't break too long or you might never finish.

On the other hand, if the words are flowing onto the page, let the phone ring, the washer wait, and the dishes drip dry. Just refill the coffee mug and keep writing.

I find I can only write approximately three pages of new text in one sitting. Often, I will write the beginning of an essay late at night, sleep on it, then wake the next morning and finish the story before starting my day.

I have made three pages my daily goal. To try

to write more would be unattainable or discouraging and to write less, for me, would be unproductive.

FINDING YOUR VOICE AND STYLE

Voice is the tone your essay takes on and *style* is the way you choose to tell your story.

Hearing your own voice or evaluating your style can be difficult. It is the reason I don't try to classify my own writing. People often ask me how I chose my style and I respond by saying, "I didn't." I don't believe you *can* choose a style.

Many professional writers recommend studying the masters for style. I do **not** agree. If you attempt to copy someone else's style, your efforts will show as superficial, awkward, inconsistent.

Your natural style will simply flow. Don't look for it. And don't force it.

If your story flows well and seems consistent and comfortable, you are likely in your own voice and have begun to develop your own style.

BONUS TIP: You cannot *copy* the voice and/or style of another writer and do it well. These come from within and surface only through writing regularly. The more you write, the more evident your voice and style become.

Voice and style are difficult concepts and I recommend you not worry about them. Don't write to win literary awards. Just tell your story and your voice will take over, your style will trickle in.

VOICE/STYLE MINI-TEST

To test the natural flow of the voice/style you've allowed to seep in, read the essay aloud and ask yourself the following questions:

- 1. Are you comfortable reading the story?
- 2. What is the mood of the piece—cold, warm?
- 3. Does the essay sound forced, awkward, or stilted?
- 4. Is it easy to read and understand?
- 5. Do you feel satisfied at the end?

STAY CLOSE TO THE STORY

When involved in the telling of a personal experience, there is a tendency for some writers to remove themselves from the story, especially if it is an emotional topic. In doing so, the essay takes on the style of a news story even when written in the first person.

The following example will illustrate how to write using emotional details to keep the reader close to the main character's perspective.

Example:

Don't write: "We packed, only what we needed, in the borrowed wagon. There was no room for my sentimental belongings."

Write: "I smoothed my calloused hand across the disintegrating pages of Grandma's journal. How could I leave this? But there was no room in the wagon for sentimental 'junk', as Jim would call it."

The first example sounds removed, distant. We don't *feel* any emotion on the part of the author.

The second example, however, has feeling.

In addition to exposing her emotional status, we learn something physical about the author with "her calloused hand". This tells us she is not pampered and perhaps works with her hands. We discover what the character cherishes—memories of Grandma.

We can, also, surmise from these 33 words that Jim, presumably her husband, is less sentimental and more practical than the author. There might even be the hint of marital problems to surface later. Was there something in the journal the author will need at the end of her journey? Will she regret not having packed it? Will she tuck it inside her jacket, risking confrontation with her husband?

BONUS TIP: By raising questions, you hold the reader's attention. This *lends depth* to the story without changing the facts—which, in the above example, encompasses the action of packing the wagon.

Stay close to your story by telling how you reacted, how you felt. Describe the impact of the happening—how it affected you, both superficially and profoundly, physically and emotionally. This approach makes your story more interesting, more believable, and more memorable for the reader. Most importantly, it makes your story **saleable**.

BONUS TIP: Be careful not to be overly emotional. Instead of saying, "I sobbed when I found Grandma's journal", let the reader *feel* the emotion. The simple act of smoothing her hand over the journal lets the reader know the character values the book and that it brings back memories.

THE SHORTER, THE BETTER

Simply because you are being more specific about thoughts and feelings, doesn't mean you should write a 10,000-word saga. Keep to the core of the story and keep it short. Essays that sell are usually 600-1200 words in length.

Unless you are Dave Barry or Erma Bombeck, you'll have a better chance of selling if you keep your writing short. Editors don't have much space or money to spend on essays. Face it, hard news sells first. As one editor I know put it, "I'd rather buy **real** stories."

PACING

One aspect of the personal essay that varies greatly from writer to writer is pacing—how quickly your story moves along. This has nothing to do with word count. It is the "speed" of the story, how rapidly events are occurring.

Given the length of most published personal essays, approximately 600-1200 words, the quicker the pacing, the better. This word count does not allow much room for detailed description or meandering thoughts. It is best to **keep your writing tight and keep the story moving**.

The following quiz will help you to decide your "pacing tendencies".

PACING QUIZ
WHAT IS YOUR COFFEE-DRINKING PACE?
What Pace Do You Prefer When You Read?

Generally, the pace of what you like to read is how you should pace your own story, at least at first. Take this quiz to find what pace you prefer.

1. When choosing a book for yourself, you...
    a. usually choose nonfiction including history, biography, instructional, or self-help books.
    b. almost always choose fiction. Rarely do you want to read about some dead guy in a powdered wig.
    c. choose magazines. You like to read, from beginning to end, in short snippets of time.

2. Regarding the page length of your chosen reading, you...
    a. look for a page-count under 200 or hope for lots of pictures.
    b. don't take the number of pages into account. You'd reach for *Les Miserables* as readily as you would *The Christmas Box*.
    c. check for short chapters. Even if the book is lengthy, you'll make it through, one chapter at a time.

3. When reading a novel you don't find interesting, you...
    a. give it 50 pages, then quit, if you're not hooked.
    b. decide to finish the book but doing so takes you much longer than usual. You'll probably complete other books before finishing this one.
    c. read to the final page even if you are not enjoying yourself. After all, a commitment is a commitment.

4. If a section of a novel is technically over your head, you...
  a. read through it a second time. If you still don't get it, you move on.
  b. read it again, more slowly, until you finally figure the meaning of the technical jargon.
  c. skip it. Who cares? You don't really need to know the details of an autopsy anyway.

5. If, suddenly, there is a character in a novel you don't recognize, you...
  a. go back through the text until you find where that character was introduced.
  b. check back to where you think you saw the name before, but if you can't find it, you forget it and read on.
  c. keep reading. You'll figure out who the new kid on the block is eventually.

6. When an author is describing the knick-knacks ornamenting the main character's shelves, you...
  a. skim.
  b. skip.
  c. plow through at your usual pace.

7. Regarding whether you would read a full-length book, either fiction or non-fiction, more than once, you...
  a. do it all the time.
  b. would never consider doing so.
  c. have done so on occasion but don't make a habit of it.

THE PACING QUIZ ANSWER SHEET

Write the letter for your answer to each question on the blank to the right. Record the letter that appears most often in the OVERALL blank at the bottom. Then, read about your pacing personality.

1.   a. S   b. I   c. G   ___S___

2.   a. G   b. S   c. I   ___S___

3.   a. G   b. I   c. S   _G_

4.   a. I   b. S   c. G   _S_

5.   a. S   b. I   c. G   _S_

6.   a. I   b. G   c. S   _I_

7.   a. S   b. G   c. I   _I_

OVERALL _____

G = GUZZLER

You like stories that read quickly, so don't bog down your essay with lots of unnecessary details. Pack it with movement toward an action-oriented climax.

S = SIPPER

You enjoy reading description and detail, so focus your essay on a shorter period of time or on a specific part of the story. This will keep the length of your work within a reasonable word count and will allow you room to *describe*!

I = INBETWEENER

You don't mind a sprinkling of description, now and then, but you don't like to be overwhelmed. Simply tell your story and allow yourself to be descriptive when you feel the urge.

Chapter Five

ADD THE CREAM AND SUGAR
ENHANCE YOUR STORY

Adding the cream—the details that thicken your story and give it depth—and the sugar—the sweet specifics that aid in making your story unique—can change a rough draft into a story that sells.

In this section, we will discuss improving the first draft of your essay—both in structure and content—while avoiding the urge to pump up your story with unbelievable untruths.

BE HONEST

Beware of the saccharin. The false statements you might be tempted to add will actually make your story too sensational. In other words, too much of the pink stuff and you'll lose credibility *and* your audience. Saying you won the Nobel Peace Prize when you merely volunteered in the neighborhood soup kitchen or claiming you lost 200 pounds when you only lost 20 is not being truthful with your reader. And believe me, they'll know.

On the other hand, it is perfectly acceptable to use literary license. This means you may edit certain facts or change them for simplicity or clarity.

Examples:

☑ If your mother's aunt's first cousin-once-removed is key in the story, simplify this by saying, "third cousin" or "distant relative", even if this is not the exact truth. Who this person is, specifically, is probably not relevant to the outcome of the story.

☑ By all means, you may accent various aspects of the story in order to make it flow better even if the events did not occur in that exact order or meet the same emphasis in real life.

The true peak of my Halloween story was when I walked through the double doors in costume and saw a bunch of plainly-clothed children. (See Appendix A.) But the build-up to that moment was mundane—it involved a lengthy conversation with my mother over which day I was supposed to wear my costume. I switched the emphasis to receiving the blue ribbon which makes for a better climax. The entrance, in costume, provides the perfect hook for the beginning of the story.

BONUS TIP: To protect yourself, change the names of anyone and everyone in your essay, even the good guys, even family members.

BEGINNINGS, MIDDLES, AND ENDINGS

I could devote a full-length book to this topic. What I have provided, instead, is an overview, but I think you'll find these tips informative and useful.

✓ Beginnings

A strong beginning grabs the reader's attention and compels him to read on. It has been said that editors read only the first few paragraphs of an unknown writer's work before moving on to the next submission. So if you have any "zing" in your story, use it in the beginning. Make each word of your opening count. It might be your only chance to interest your editor of choice.

A gripping opening might make the fundamental difference between a well-written essay that sells and a good story that doesn't.

❖ **Start late**. For your beginning, start telling the story as *late* as possible. In other words, begin as close to the climax as you can, giving little background information. Your reader isn't interested in how you got to where you were going. He wants to know what happened once you arrived.

Be sure to begin your story at the **moment of change** and not before. This would be the moment when your bad day became chaotic or when your gnawing pain became an attack.

BONUS TIP: Remember to open your essay at the moment when the trying situation became unbearable or the silly moment escalated to hysterical.

BONUS TIP: This technique is difficult to master. In order to "get into" your story as a writer, you might *have* to write down the insignificant details which serve to propel you into the story. You can

omit them, later. I often end up cutting the first two paragraphs of my initial drafts.

❖ **Hook** the audience with a clever saying, a twist, a play on words, an interesting personal event, or a situation to which many people can relate.
Example:
In "The Turkey's Wingless Flight", an essay about when my husband and I were on a Florida vacation for the Thanksgiving holiday, the first paragraph ends with "More critically, we'd miss our mothers. Without them, who would cook the Thanksgiving turkey?"

Just about everyone has a kitchen horror story. This opening hooks the reader, causing her to settle in and compare your turkey story with hers.
❖ **Answer** the following simple questions in your opening: Who is speaking? What is the setting? What dilemma does the character face?

State the problem of the story by the second or third paragraph. Disclose it clearly, in one or two simple sentences. Answer: Why is this particular happening worthy of the reader's attention?
Example:
The opening of my essay, "By Candlelight", reads, "Although I'm quite accustomed to the modern conveniences of computers and laser printers, I wrote this longhand—with a pencil—on the back of my daughter's crayon portrait of a spider, by candlelight. By candlelight on an empty Sunday night, late. No incandescent, fluorescent, nor any other kind of luminescence. No kidding. No choice."

I have answered the three key questions in these first 54 words. It is obvious I am a mother, in my home, facing the trials of being stuck without electricity.

❖ **Drizzle in your background information**, a phrase at a time. Don't give all your uninteresting, yet necessary, facts in consecutive paragraphs. You'll lose your focus *and* your reader.

Remember your audience—whether it be comprised of an editor or reader—is impatient by nature and will only give you a few paragraphs to prove yourself. If you succeed in your beginning, the reader will finish the story. If you fail, she will move on to someone else's well-written work.

BEGINNING MINI-TEST

Have you answered the following in your beginning?
- 1. Who is talking? What type of person are you? Age? Sex? Classification—mother, cowboy, business person?
- 2. Where are you?
- 3. What is the problem?

✓ Middles

Perfecting the middle of your story is the most difficult part of essay writing. Use these guidelines to plow through to an exciting climax.

❖ **Tension** must increase throughout the middle of your essay in order to hold the reader's interest and propel him toward the climax and the end of the story.

Each event must build on the last and be relevant to the climax and theme.

BONUS TIP: Read through the story and draw breaks on your copy where one segment or thought ends and the next begins. Do any developments draw the reader away from where you are headed, distracting from the climax?   Are any sections bothersome? Is each point necessary?

If any point seems out of place, attempt to find where it might better fit into the story.   If the particular happening doesn't increase the tension and does nothing to support the overall point you are attempting to make, omit it completely.

❖ **There must be change** as the reader progresses through the middle of the story.   The character cannot remain the same throughout the essay. He must experience some kind of evolution, whether it be positive or negative.

❖ **Show depth** of character.   Give your character dimension by disclosing details about his motivation and intentions.   Divulge what he is thinking and why.

Example:

In my Halloween essay, at the beginning, we think we know who the character is—a child who made a silly mistake by dressing up on the wrong day. In the middle, we discover she is actually a strong individual with self-confidence and direction. This gives the character depth and makes her likable to the reader.

❖ **Head toward the unveiling** or relevance of your story. Approach the revelation, the climax, the point of your telling the story.

Examples:

✅ You have proven yourself to be a strong individual.

✅ You admit you're in love with your dance instructor.

✅ You believe holding a grudge is wrong.

The middle of your story must keep the reader reading. If you don't build in tension and keep dishing out relevant information, you reader will yawn and doze off. Be certain to stay focused. Keep on track by eliminating any points that stray from your theme.

MIDDLE MINI-TEST

Have you covered the following throughout the middle of your essay?

- 1. Is each point necessary to the climax or turning point in the story? Does each explain the relevance of the story or reveal more about the character?
- 2. Does each point build in tension in an ascending order, toward the climax? If not, rearrange.
- 3. Did you skim past or dread reading any section in particular? If so, change or omit.

✓ **Endings**

Upon reading your ending, the reader should sigh with relief, cry with compassion, or smile with delight. You must summarize and bring the story to a close. Above all else, your ending must satisfy.

BONUS TIP: It is acceptable and desirable to leave the reader questioning. Does she agree with the author? Could she be a better person? Is our prison system unjust? Are we headed toward another recession?

❖ **Tie up loose ends**. If you mention something once, no matter how minor, it is best to address that point at least once more. As a rule, I think twice is enough, three times at the most. I like to think of this technique as pleasing the reader's subconscious.
  Examples:
    ✓ In "The Ears of Halloween", I had a change of clothes with me in a green duffle bag. If I had carried the bag in the beginning, then never used it, the reader would have thought, why mention it? Or if I had, all of a sudden, pulled clothes from a duffle bag, readers would have thought, now where did that come from? To resolve this, the duffle bag is mentioned three times in the essay.
    ✓ If you told the reader your mother was in the hospital earlier, we must know how mother is doing by the end of the essay.
    ❖ **Resolve the problem** or at least fully address the situation. Don't leave the reader wondering, what was the outcome? Let him know how the character escaped the predicament.

❖ **The conclusion should be significant**, momentous, if not earth-shattering.

Example:

You dressed up on the wrong day. It affected your entire life.

❖ **The ending should summarize** the story, even if only in a sentence or two. Review what happened and comment on the outcome. Sometimes, if the writer gets bogged down with the theme and the message, he neglects to finish telling the story.

Example:

In the Halloween essay, the last paragraph begins, "Although I don't dress up on the wrong day anymore, I still make mistakes."

This simple statement summarizes the story.

❖ **Add a twist.** An ending is *more* than satisfying if it involves a twist—a surprise—something with a little "Wow!" after the climax.

BONUS TIP: The climax is often *predictable* yet still satisfying while the twist is *unpredictable*, unexpected.   Catching the reader off guard is an extremely effective technique. If you can master this, you're as good as published!

A strong ending leaves the reader with something—he either questions the result or agrees with it.

The character, you, should have changed throughout the body of the essay and the reader should change as a result of reading your story.

ENDING MINI-TEST

Answer the following questions about your ending:

- 1. Do you feel satisfied, or is something about the essay not quite right?
- 2. Check your minor points. Have you re-addressed them all? Have you left any gnawing particulars unanswered?
- 3. Is the ending momentous and significant, or is it trivial and irrelevant?

NOTE: Rachel Simon, in her book, *The Writer's Survival Guide*, brings up an excellent point. I have paraphrased:

The climax is tied to character while the realization at the end is tied to theme.

Example:

Again, in the Halloween essay, the *character* shows strength at the *climax* after dressing up on wrong day and receiving the blue ribbon.

The realization at the *end* is that we must remain strong, unique, and grow as a result of our mistakes. This is the fundamental *theme* of the essay.

THE TRICK LIST: 15 WAYS TO ENHANCE YOUR WRITING

What follows is a list of tricks I use to enhance my writing and add depth to my story. Overall, the tricks should be used sparingly and by no means should all of these show up in any one writing. That would be overwhelming for all—writer, editor and reader, alike.

These tricks are compiled from my own experience—this is what works for me. I am confident if you drizzle these into your writing effectively and sparingly, you will have editors commenting on the quality and uniqueness of your writing style.

✓Be Clever, But Don't Overdo It

While it is effective to include plays on words in your work or to link clever terms to the underlying theme, too much of this will cause the reader to groan. As a writer, you want to get through to the reader or editor but you don't want to get under her skin.

Example:

In one of my essays, entitled "Group", about my writer's critique group, I changed the names of the people to nouns or adjectives that captured some aspect of their personalities. One woman was a coffee drinker, so her name became "Coffee". Another was a former water softener salesperson, and he became "Water". A third member was a recently divorced mother of two. Her assigned nick-name was "Free", and so on.

At one point in the essay, I say "Coffee seemed to perk up." Now, this is imaginative, but suppose what followed was "Water drowned in anticipation and Free liberated her spirits, while Nurse administered and Dark gloomed." Each phrase, alone, is clever but, together, the effect is overdone.

To overuse the technique becomes cutsie and annoying.

BONUS TIP: Don't use this trick every time a character is mentioned.   Take "Coffee", for example. After he perks up, he could *brew*, *steam*, and *grow bitter with time,* but this weakens the effectiveness of the original idea.

✓ Use Opposites

Use opposite terms in consecutive sentences or in two parts of the same sentence for emphasis.

Example:

✓ In one essay, called "Shrinking Necessities", I had heard about a study in which scientists discovered when women are pregnant, their brains shrink. An excerpt goes as follows:

"Somehow, the whole idea didn't seem fair. While every other inch of my body was **swelling**—including the fingers, the cellulite, and the sinuses—the one organ I needed most was **shrinking**. The brain."

✓ In another essay, called "The St. Valentine's Day Sleighing", I used opposites to emphasize a chaotic moment—sliding down the mountain in an old station wagon. It was written as follows:

"We assumed crash positions in the vehicle, swerving, skidding and, somehow, dodging **large** trees and **small** animals."

✓ Repeat Phrases

I invite you to repeat words or phrases in

consecutive sentences or in two parts of the same sentence for emphasis. This tends to make the piece more lyrical and allows it to flow better.

Example:

In my essay, called "Masked Revenge", I wore an ape costume to startle my husband on Halloween.

"The rubber shoes and gloves fit as if made from casts of my own feet and hands. I shivered. **This was** eerie. **This was** exciting."

This basic technique can be quite effective if used properly and sparingly. Repeat too often and the editor will think you forgot to edit your work.

✓ Ask Questions

Every now and then, turn an emphatic statement into a question. This works well at particularly intense moments, at times of decision, and in the summarizing statements.

Example:

In my essay, "Masked Revenge", my husband kept pulling the same pranks on me. Instead of writing, "This trick wasn't funny anymore. And I was so angry I couldn't tell when he was going to pull it on me," the piece asks, "How could he continue to find humor in this trick? And why did I continue to fall for it?"

Note how the word "continue" is repeated for effect. (See "Repeat Phrases", above.)

Using this technique will catch the reader's attention and bring her closer to the story. It is almost as if you are addressing the reader, personally, without disrupting the flow of the story.

✓ Use Simple, Visual Similes and Metaphors

Choose similes and metaphors which are openly relevant and easy for the reader to visualize or relate to. Don't try to be too abstract or overly symbolic. This might confuse or frustrate your audience.

Examples:

✓ In my essay about the diminishing brain called "Shrinking Necessities", the similes I use might seem silly, but they fit the mood of the piece which is upbeat and humorous. One example reads,

"These are the same people whose babies bonded better than Kenyan monkeys."

✓ In the essay, "The Turkey's Wingless Flight", I used several visual similes.

"In the airport, people stared and pointed. We looked like a team of surgeons carrying an organ for transplant. I couldn't have guessed that a cooler containing a thawing turkey—which wasn't getting any lighter—would attract so much attention. It must have been the reason for our hailing a cab so quickly, even from the back of the line."

And later in the piece when the turkey is sprawled out in the pan, I write, "Something wasn't right. The turkey had moved. He lay open-armed as if to invite me into the pan.

'Ooo,' I yelped."

✓ In my essay, "holocaust", I used an analogy to frame the story (see "Frame the Story", below), which means I began and ended the essay using the following images:

"I watched as my daughters pretended to wash their Barbie® doll clothes. They undressed each doll and stacked it in a pile to the side. I had observed this ritual many times before, but it had never disturbed me like it did this time. As the stack grew, I squeezed my eyes shut and turned my head.

"The mound of flesh-colored appendages overlapped to the point where it became difficult to distinguish which arms and legs belonged to which doll. Expressionless faces blended together in a harrowing collage, bringing to mind a vivid and horrible picture—the stacks of life wasted, so desperately, during the holocaust."

I entered this essay in a writing contest and received several comments on the opening. One judge wrote, "Very original lead with Barbie® dolls" and another jotted, "The doll image is excellent. Best part of piece."

✓ Frame the Story

The above example, also, illustrates the technique of framing a story. The essay opens and closes with some analogy or idea that is **not** woven throughout the body of the text. In fact, it is generally not even referred to, other than at the beginning and ending.

Example:

In the "holocaust" essay (the beginning can be found in the "Simile" section above), the ending is as follows:

"In unrestrained joy, my daughters giggled over their toys, snapping me back to the moment. As I watched them stack their naked Barbie® dolls, I knew I would, one day, take them there, to the Holocaust

Museum. Not because they will ever meet a victim's family member or recognize a survivor, but because they are Americans and they should know. They should feel the effect. They should question how this could have happened in their grandparent's lifetime.

"And like me, they should always remember."

✓ Use Exaggeration

Stretching the truth or overstating points through exaggeration works best in humorous or light-hearted essays.

Example:

In my essay, "Shrinking Necessities", I write, "It was this same group of people whose kids walked at four months, talked at six months, and were accepted 'Early Admission' to Harvard."

This example shows an appropriate amount of exaggeration—a stretch beyond the truth but not too far. Don't go to the extreme or you'll find you're writing slapstick.

✓ Single Out a Sentence as a Separate Paragraph

Singling out a short sentence or phrase from the rest of the text and placing it as its own paragraph is an effective way to accent the point at hand. As the break stops the reader's eye, the tightness of the phrase creates a kind of staccato reaction, causing the reader to *pay attention*.

Example:

In the essay, "Masked Revenge", I write,

"She was a neighbor who enjoyed playing pranks as much as my husband and was equally competent at pulling them off.

"Unlike me."

"Unlike me" is a simple phrase—not even a complete sentence—which serves to summarize the entire theme of the story. The main character is not good at playing tricks on others and does so on her husband with reluctance.

✓ Surprise, Then Explain

Even though the trick worked in *The Wizard of Oz*, few people like to be fooled for very long. I suggest throwing in a surprise, now and then, but recommend explaining it in the same paragraph or the next. No more waking up at the end and finding it's all a dream. That's cheating.

Examples:

✓ In my essay, "Masked Revenge", I dressed in a gorilla costume and rang the front door bell to trick my husband. What follows is how I surprised the reader, then explained:

"As he turned toward the basement once again, I pounced on his back and gnawed at his neck with my rubber lips.

"But he didn't react. Because I had only attacked in the deep recesses of my imagination.

"Yes, ultimately I had chickened out. Right there on the spot. Instead of an aggressive gorilla laying one on my husband's neck, I was a meek monkey and removed the mask."

For a short time, the reader is surprised this reluctant gorilla would attack anyone. In the next paragraph, the reader finds he was right—the gorilla didn't attack, after all.

✓In the final paragraph of "The Turkey's Wingless Flight", the two had finished dinner and were discussing the cooking of their first turkey.

"In the end, we vowed never to roast another turkey on Thanksgiving—without first removing its flapping wings."

For a moment, the reader is surprised the two will not roast another turkey after their successful initial attempt. Later in the sentence, he finds they will—but not without, first, cutting off its wings. The surprise and the explanation are both within the same sentence.

✓ Come Full-Circle

Coming full-circle is the simple concept of tying the end of the story back in with something that was mentioned in the opening. I don't use all of the techniques, mentioned here, in each essay, but I *do* use this one, without fail.

What coming full-circle does is give a feeling of completion, of conclusion, of closure. It is satisfying to the reader to have a link between the hook—that kept them reading in the beginning—and the end, where everything comes together. This technique causes the reader to think, "Wow, she began her story with that same idea."

Example:

In the essay I wrote about having no electricity for 27 hours, called "By Candlelight", I open and close with the idea of writing by candlelight. The first paragraph reads:

"Although I'm quite accustomed to the modern conveniences of computers and laser printers, I wrote this longhand—with a pencil—on the back of my daughter's crayon portrait of a spider.

"By candlelight."

After the electricity is restored, the end reads:

"With that—and this dull pencil—the creative juices began to flow.

"And in time, the electrical juices started to flow, as well. But instead of fiddling with the remote control or gulping the iced tea I'd craved for hours, I curled up on the couch, flipped off the switch and finished writing this.

"By candlelight."

NOTE: **Notice how "By Candlelight" is not a complete sentence but is singled out as a separate paragraph for emphasis.** (See "Single Out a Sentence as a Separate Paragraph", earlier in this section.)

✓ Use Alliteration

Most readers are impressed when a writer is able to relate two or more **useful**, appropriate words beginning with the same sound. You may also repeat vowel or consonants sounds in the *middle* or at the *end* of the words.

This is an eighth-grade technique but it's surprising how few writers use the tool well. If you can maintain the true meaning of what you intended without forcing words to fit the format, this is a handy, effective way to "show off". It is crucial, though, not to sacrifice meaning or emphasis. Alliteration only works if it fits and if it flows.

Example:

In my essay about losing the electricity, called "By Candlelight", I write:

"No incandescent, fluorescent, nor any other kind of luminescence. No kidding. No choice."

This demonstrates alliteration, repeating the "s" sound within the words. I could have written, "No white light, no fluorescence, no bulbs at all." But it would have been much less effective.

✓ **Use the Magical Rule of Three**

Rhythmically, a list of three objects, actions, or thoughts is more lyrical than a list of two or four. And whether you realize it or not, your prose *should* have rhythm to keep a pleasing flow to the story. If a sentence seems awkward to you, it probably is. Follow your intuition and change it, perhaps by using the magical rule of three.

Example:

In the essay, "By Candlelight", after I finally *accept* the loss of electricity, it reads:

"The peace was comfortable. **No answering machine, no low-budget commercials, no reason to do laundry.** The rhythmic breathing of my daughters in slumber at my sides was calming.

A kind of Henry David Thoreau moment—a time to ponder **truth, profound love and the meaning of light**…"

Mini-Exercise:
Read the above lists of three, subtracting one of the three or adding another. Notice how, when only two are read, you hesitate, waiting for more. When four are read, you become monotone and lose the focus. There is a natural rhythm to a list of three. And it's an easy technique to master.

BONUS TIP: Try adding alliteration to the Rule of Three for an enhanced lyrical flow. (See "Use Alliteration" example above.)

✓ Choose a Theme

It is important to weave a thread through your story. This is advice you've heard before, I'm certain, but it is amazing how few writers actually support a theme consistently throughout. To make this effective, you must relate all major happenings to that theme, as well as associate your word choices with the theme chosen. Keep coming back to the underlying theme—the true meaning behind the essay—without overdoing it, and your work will be tight, relevant, salable.

Example:
In my essay, called "The Saint Valentine's Day Sleighing", about my husband and I going on a sleigh ride in the mountains, the theme throughout is the question "Was it romantic?" At several points in the essay, I ask that question. The answer varies depending upon what is happening at that moment in the story. (See Appendix B.) Most every point in the essay either strongly, or remotely, supports the theme.

All events are linked, which makes the essay flow well and read easily.

✓ Use the Weather

It is important to let the reader know the main character's environment, however brief.

Example:

If a character suffers from a lack of energy and motivation in the dead of winter, the reader might not be alarmed. It is common for even the most emotionally stable of people to suffer the winter doldrums.

But if the character wants to sleep excessively and doesn't want to leave the house in the late spring when the wind is warm, the flowers are in bloom and the sun is bright overhead, the reader is alerted to the fact that the character might be clinically depressed. The only difference, here, is the weather.

Once again, don't go into heavy detail. Simply add a phrase, here and there, to give fullness to the essay. It is relevant the hear how "the wind pressed against her" but not to read "the wind blew down from the northwest at approximately 55 miles per hour in a swirl that touched seven states in less that twelve hours."

BONUS TIP: Sprinkle in the secondary information. Don't send it in showers.

✓ Use the Senses

Incorporate sensory information into your essay. Include snippets of detail about the sights, smells, sounds, tastes and feel of what's around you. Add the squeal of sausage in the pan or the tickle of dangle earrings on your neck. Using this technique makes your essay tangible. It gives the reader something to grasp, helps him picture the scene, experience the event.

Again, you want to use this technique sparingly. Too much talk about the sound of waves crashing or the feel of chinchilla will distract your audience from the point of the story.

We describe sights often, telling others the details of a niece's wedding gown or the colors of rock in the Grand Canyon. We talk about tastes, too, when we describe the meal we had at a new restaurant. Hearing, touch and sound are a bit more difficult to describe and, in daily conversation, we seem to get little practice doing so.

SMELL EXERCISE

This exercise was designed to help you improve your description of how things smell. Really think about the essence of the smell. What memories does it stir? What feelings does it arouse? Attempt to use words you wouldn't use in average conversation. Is the smell pungent, mild, overwhelming, faint? Be specific. Get personal. Does it remind you of something in particular?

Place the following on a nearby table and smell each, one at a time:

Vinegar, Vicks VapoRub®, perfume, pine scented cleaning fluid, suntan lotion.

Describe the essence of the smell, its effect. Jot down simple words, phrases, or complete sentences. Refer to specific instances in your past brought to mind by the smell. Use similes or metaphors.

Your nose might need a break after the first three smells.

SAMPLE ANSWERS

1. **Vinegar**: sour; tingly; reverberates the nasal membrane; like grandpa's oak pickle barrel.

2. **Vicks VapoRub®**: cool warmth; inner cleansing; like a burning eucalyptus bush.

3. **Perfume**: spicy; musky; natural oils; like a brewing pot of sweetened herbs and dew-dipped petals.

4. **Pine Scent**: like a mixture of Clorox and cheap air freshener; like a sterilized hospital room.

5. **Suntan Lotion**: like a Caribbean breeze over darkened, oiled skin.

SENSORY EXERCISE

Give yourself time when doing exercises concerning the senses. This is difficult work, for you are moving into uncharted waters. Write down your answers in your essay notebook. They will come in handy when you are working on an essay and are stumped on how to describe the feel or sound of something.

Keep an open mind and begin.

62 *Write Well & Sell*

1. For more practice on **sight** description, take five photos from your drawer. Pick ones that are *not* similar, e.g. a family reunion, a child's face, a person swinging or running or splashing, a landscape, a sporting event, etc. Try to describe differences in expression, coloring, and actions. Extrapolate to cover possible intentions: What happened after the picture was taken? Did the group break up? Did the runner stumble? What was the subject thinking?

2. For practice on **touch**, gather some household objects e.g. cotton balls, pebbles, feathers, sand, bath towels, etc. Feel each in your hand, one at a time. Brush each over the back of your hand or against your cheek. Think about weight, texture, effect. Try to go beyond conventional descriptions.
   Example:
   When people think of cotton balls they think "soft". When I touch a cotton ball, I think "sticky". Why? Because, in the winter, my hands are dry and the threads of cotton get caught on the rough, dry skin.

3. For practice on **sounds**, listen to the noises you make daily, e.g. ripping paper, ringing the phone, pouring liquid. At a critical moment in an essay, these simple sounds can be magnified for effect. Do the sounds delight you, frighten you, excite you? Think about their impact.
   Example:
   The sound of paper ripping could encompass the joy of opening a gift or the frustration of tearing up an unwanted letter. Both give a distinctly different image to the reader.

4. **Taste** is an easy one. Practice describing the food you eat but go one step further. Try a food you don't normally eat or don't enjoy. How does it feel on your tongue? Is there an aftertaste? What is it about the taste that does not appeal to you?
   Example:
   To me, pickled red beets have the aftertaste of dirt or soil.

5. To top it all off, choose one thing and describe all aspects of it using the senses. For example, use coffee or your favorite beverage. How does it look, smell, sound, taste, and feel?

Calling the reader's attention to the little things they see, hear, smell, touch and do everyday has a dramatic effect. It can change the impact of your essay, heighten it, deepen it. It leaves the reader in awe saying, "I have never thought about the sound of pouring coffee."

THE IMPORTANCE OF TITLES

There is no doubt a title can make or break a piece. Readers, if interested or intrigued by a title, will read on. If offended, confused or unmoved by a title, a reader will move on to read someone else's work.

What follows are tips on finding the appropriate title.

✓ Write All Possible Titles

If a title comes to you, either for an essay you are currently working on, one you have completed, or one you want to write, jot it down on an index card or in a notebook. Even if you already have a working title for the item, jot down additional ideas. You never know which one will best fit the final form of the essay.

✓ Use Clever Twists

If you think of a clever twist on words or a unique way of saying something, jot it down, too, even if it is unrelated to any of your essay ideas at the time.

Examples:

✓ I wrote an essay about celebrating the New Year at 10:00 pm, not midnight, and entitled it, "Premature Celebration".

✓ My Thanksgiving essay, about carrying a frozen turkey on the airplane with us and, then, chopping off its wings before baking, was entitled, "The Turkey's Wingless Flight".

✓ The title of my Valentine essay, "The St. Valentine's Day Sleighing", was a twist on the St. Valentine's Day Massacre substituting "Sleighing" which sounds like "Slaying". It's a little remote, but it worked and it sold.

✓ Use Double Meanings.

Use familiar phrases or clichés in the title, but with some change or double meaning.

Examples:

✓ My essay about my reluctance to serve as a juror in a criminal trial was entitled, "All Rise".

✓ In "A Mother's Memorial", about my grandmother's loss of a son, the words of the title have multiple meanings. My grandmother's birthday was on **Memorial Day**, she always remembered her son who was killed in the war on **Memorial Day**, and I—now, a **mother**, like her—am offering a **memorial** to my grandmother and my uncle by writing the essay.

✓ Use an Intriguing Combination of Words.

For still more title ideas, use intriguing combinations of words that would not normally appear together in a sentence.

Example:

In "The Ears of Halloween", *ears* make the reader think of rabbit ears and Easter. In combination with *Halloween,* this might leave the reader asking, "What is the connection here?" If he thinks, he could surmise that the title likely deals with a Halloween costume. Had it been "The Ears of Christmas", it might have been too vague and the editors would have probably asked me to change it.

✓ Keep It Short.

As a rule, I like short titles. In this rapidly-paced world, readers want to see a title and interpret it quickly. So avoid long titles and subtitles for personal essays. One-word titles can be quite emphatic.

Example:

✓ Calling my essay about my writer's critiquing meetings, "Group" is more effective than a title like, "A Unique Group of People" and much more intriguing than "My Writer's Group". Just "Group" might have readers asking, "It is it some kind of group therapy?"—which it is, in a way.

✓ In my title, "holocaust", a sense of starkness is conveyed by the singularity of the word and the lack of capitalization.

✓ Don't Give It Away.

Be sure not to give too much away with the title or make it too obvious. One of my favorite things to do is to interpret what a title means and to figure why the author chose the title she did. I love the revelation, but if it is too obvious or comes too soon, I'm disappointed.

Example:

My essay entitled "Second Election, First Lesson" was about my sixth-grade experience. I won the election for Class President in September and, come January, the teacher decided to hold another election. My term was originally to be for a full year. I won again, but the **second election** became my **first lesson** in how, for whatever reason, life isn't always fair.

Think of a catchy, clever, or intriguing word or group of words for your title. Whatever you do, spend time on it. Think it through. The title is what initially impresses or turns off your editor of choice.

Chapter Six

SIP & SAVOR
EDIT & IMPROVE

The first draft is not the only *creative* part of essay writing. It is the *editing* that separates the well-written essay from the mediocre. It's what makes your story *publishable*.

How do you know what to change in a story to make it better? How can you tell if you've made your point clearly? How will you know if your essay is publishable?

The answer to the last question is...you won't. All you can do is make the story the best it can possibly be. Edit until your story is perfect, or as close to perfect as you can get.

Few editors edit anymore, rarely telling you how to improve your story. They simply reject it, if it isn't quite right. Remember, they can afford to do this because they have a stack of other writers' essays making up their slush piles.

You must edit your own work to sell it. **Make your essay unforgettable. Make it irresistible.**

BONUS TIP: When editing your work, learn to listen to your inner voice. If you don't like a certain paragraph or are uncomfortable with a passage, change it. How many times have you said to yourself, "It looks like rain," and you leave without your umbrella, anyway. Don't end up drenched in an essay you're not happy with. Change it when your instincts tell you to do so.

The following list of recommendations will help you recognize what sections to change in your essay and how to do so. This is a compilation of what works for me. If you apply these suggestions, I am certain you will carry your story from *average* to *outstanding*. That's the best you can do. Nothing can guarantee a sale, but by sending out only your best work, you'll likely receive more checks and fewer rejections.

READ ALOUD

As you read your story aloud, you will notice certain words, phrases or entire paragraphs which nag at your subconscious. You'll stumble on a specific group of words or will dread reading individual sections. **You must read aloud several times** before these inconsistencies become evident. Listen to your inner voice which is subtly telling you, "This part doesn't work."

BONUS TIP: Mark those sections with a colored pen—pencil smears and black ink doesn't stand out. You want to be sure to remember which parts of the story must be edited.

If you have an idea, right then, about how to improve it, write it in the margin and keep going. Make up your own editing marks, ones that make sense to you. (See "Don't Stop" Section in Chapter Four for a few of mine.) Continue until you have read through the entire essay four or five times.

Then change the parts you've marked.

BONUS TIP: Don't try to explain to yourself why you shouldn't edit or why you feel attached to a paragraph, sentence or phrase. If a section is bothering you, it will annoy the editor, too. If it isn't right, it must be changed.

WRITE DOWN THE OPTIONS

If you are experiencing difficulty in writing a particular section, re-write it two or three different ways. Read the changes aloud within the body of the text. Choose the one you are most comfortable with and move on to the next margin mark.

If one word is the problem, try reading aloud, replacing the word with several synonyms. Sometimes a simile or metaphor works better. Play around with it. And always, always read aloud.

FOCUS

While reading aloud, ask yourself, have I focused on the specifics? Have I avoided generalizations? Generalizations are **not** interesting and are **not** memorable. Specifics are more touching, moving, impressive. Let the reader know *exactly* what's going on.

Examples:

✓ In my essay about losing the electricity, called "By Candlelight", I include the specifics the loss had denied me.

Instead of writing, "Every electrical appliance in the house wouldn't work," I wrote, "Perspiration formed on my upper lip as I realized the cooling system no longer functioned. Neither did the VCR, nor the iced tea maker. I was shut off from all that was necessary to sustain life. So, I hung my head in the dark. And sipped water."

The specifics, here, heighten the despair and the humor, allowing the reader to better relate to the situation.

✓ In an essay, entitled "A Mother's Memorial", about my coming to understand my grandmother's decision not to bury her son in Arlington National Cemetery, I wrote specifically about how my father was informed of his brother's death.

"From aboard his ship stationed in the South Pacific, Dad wrote a letter to Frank, who was about to leave for Europe. In one sentence, Dad praised him for being a capable, strong man. In the next, he played big brother, warning Frank to be good while away from home.

"A short time later, Dad's second letter to his younger brother was returned, unopened, with a single word stamped over the address: DECEASED.

"I cannot speak of how Dad, at age 22—a man

so young, himself, and so far away from home—might have reacted at the sight of the returned letter. He never really said. And I suppose that told enough."

By focusing on the specifics, this brings the reader closer to the story, allowing him to *feel* the emotion.

Later, in the same essay, I wrote, "As a mother now, I no longer question why Grandma kept a silent vigil and an unlocked door for the son who would never return..."

By focusing on the "unlocked door", I have revealed much about the type of woman Grandma was, and how deeply she longed for her lost son.

THE DON'TS LIST: 11 MISTAKES TO AVOID

By eliminating the following from your writing, you will improve the quality and salability of your essays.

✓ Don't Preach

It is easy to get carried away with your subject, jump on a pedestal and become didactic. This is not recommended. No one wants to feel like she's being taught a lesson or being told what to do. Especially an adult. She is reading your essay primarily for enjoyment and possibly to broaden her overall scope of things—to look at the world through different eyes, your eyes.

Avoid unwanted moralizing. Don't *tell* the reader your message. *Show* her what you want her to know through the happenings and circumstances played out in the body of your essay.

I tend to get preachy at the end of my first drafts. I allow it to happen and continue to write without stopping. (See "Don't Stop" section in Chapter Four.) These *lessons* are the first things I cut in my editing process.

✓ Don't Repeat

Earlier I recommended you repeat the use of certain words, for effect, but you must do so sparingly. (See "Repeat Phrases" in Chapter Five.) Sometimes repeating a word is emphatic. Other times it's annoying. Often in a first draft, a writer will repeat a word so as not to break the flow of her writing by stopping to use a thesaurus or by thinking of an alternate way to phrase something.

Example:

In the first draft of my essay entitled "A Flicker of Fate", I used the word "flicker" again and again. One section read:

"It took me several miles to understand. The light had never **flickered** before. It didn't **flicker** while I was trying to find out why it had **flickered**. It didn't **flicker** after I put down the papers."

It now reads:

"It took me several miles to understand. The light had never **been temperamental** before. It didn't **waver** while I tried to find out why it had **flickered**. It didn't **falter** after I put down the papers."

✓ Don't Use Exclamation Points!

This is a sure sign of an amateur. Your *words* should indicate that the character is excited, surprised, overwhelmed. Using an exclamation point is cheating. It is *telling* the reader this is a stimulating section instead of *showing* him through creative word choice.

Example:

In "The St. Valentine's Day Sleighing", instead of: "We skidded the entire way up the mountain!" It reads: "My head jerked as we began our seemingly interminable sideways spinning skid up the treacherous mountainside path. Eventually, despite my furrowed brows, squeezed-shut eyelids and translucent knuckles, I sensed level ground."

It is understood that this is a moment of nervousness and fear on the part of the character. No exclamation point is necessary.

✓ Minimize Use of "to be" Verbs

Am, is, are, was, were, be, being, been are non-specific, uncreative, easy-way-out type words and readers tend to skim right over them. Take the time to use verbs with meaning and punch.

Example:

Don't write: "I **was** in the middle of the Atlantic. But I **wasn't** on a cruise ship or an ocean liner. I **was** on an upside-down life raft. There **was** no food or water. I **was** getting hot and thirsty."

Instead, write: "In the middle of the Atlantic, I **clung** to the overturned, inflatable raft. I **fought** the urge to scream. Without food or water, I **needed** to conserve energy, to maintain strength. As the heat of the sun **robbed** my lips of moisture, I **licked** them. I **tried** to think, to plan, when I **sensed** a thickness in my throat and a swelling of my tongue. Mere swallowing had become strenuous."

✓ Avoid *-ing*

The use of words ending in *-ing* slows the pace of your story. Instead of writing, "*while he was sleeping*", write "*while he slept*".

✓ Avoid Clichés

This is one of my biggest pet-peeves. In speech, using clichés—or familiar, overused phrases and "common" ways to say things—is acceptable. As a writer, you must omit the use of *all* clichés in your essays. This includes, not only sayings like "A bird in the hand...", but common phrases like, "same old thing" or "dead on arrival".

Take the basic idea behind the cliché you want to use and change it. Try to think of a new way to say the same thing. Even "I love you" can be considered a cliché.

Example:

Don't write: "The **old guy** finally **kicked the bucket**. Too bad he got his **bell rung** and ended up **seeing stars**. If he'd have gone to the hospital, he probably wouldn't have **cooked his own goose**. I guess he was afraid of getting **taken to the cleaners**."

Instead, write: "Mr. **Collagen** finally **pounded the pail**. It saddened me to hear about his head injury and the hallucinations. If he'd have gone to the hospital, he probably wouldn't have **baked his own chicken**. I suppose he feared being **taxied to the laundromat**."

I wouldn't advise using this many clever twists in one paragraph, however. It becomes confusing. Be sure the meaning of your twisted cliché is "crystal clear"—or should I say "clear as grandma's goblets in the summer sun"?

✓ Avoid Ellipses and Parentheses

Editors don't care for either of these forms of breaking up sentences. Ellipses... are often used in place of a pause. It is better to use a dash—which consists of two hyphens on your typewriter or computer keyboard.

Parentheses (too directed toward the reader) break the flow of the essay. The use of parentheses interrupts the telling of the story in order to address the reader directly. This is distracting and might cause the reader to lose focus.

The use of dashes is more acceptable—and more appealing—for both editors and readers.

✓ Use Adverbs Sparingly

These words, usually ending in -*ly*, are used to qualify verbs, adjectives or other adverbs. Some writers get carried away using these simple words which "cheat" at getting your point across.

Remember, there is nothing creative about using an adverb.

Instead, attempt to use more creative, descriptive verbs, adjectives, similes and metaphors.

Choose the word that best describes what you want to say. Writing something effectively, descriptively without the use of adverbs separates you—the publishable—from the amateurs.

Examples:

✓ Instead of **ran quickly**, you could substitute **raced, bolted, darted, sprinted, dashed, hurried, etc.**

In place of **walked slowly**, you could write **inched, strolled, sauntered, moseyed, ambled, drifted, meandered, etc.**

✓ Don't write: "She sang **beautifully** as the congregation waited **patiently** for the minister to arrive **promptly**."

Instead, write: "Her voice **like a songbird** (simile) filled the church as the congregation **anticipated** (descriptive verb) the arrival of the **ever-punctual** (descriptive adjective) priest."

✓ Don't Misuse the Thesaurus

A thesaurus is an invaluable tool but it must be used correctly. You can't simply substitute one word for another in a sentence because the meaning might not be *exactly* the same. In addition, the words preceding or following the new word must "go with" your substituted word. If you are unfamiliar with the new word, don't use it. Find a word with which you are comfortable.

Example:

I will *pay* you tomorrow.

Most verbs you would choose to substitute for *pay*, require some additional clarification in the sentence in order to make sense.

I will *give* you *the money* tomorrow.

I will *grant* you *your due monies* tomorrow.

I will *hand over the cash* tomorrow.

I will *proffer my payment* tomorrow.

I will *spend* you—even though *spend* is in the Roget's Thesaurus, it cannot be used in this application.

BONUS TIP: It is worse to use a new word improperly than to repeat a familiar term.

✓ Don't Use "You"

This is a rule you will see broken quite often. When the author writes, "And **I** realized **I** would never make the same mistake again. **You**, too, should be leery of walking down dark alleys at night," it stops me. It seems as if the author has jumped out of the essay and into a conversation with me. I prefer to concentrate on the story and draw from it what I will. I don't relish the condescending feeling the use of "you" evokes.

✓ Don't Use the Overused

Don't use commonly overused words like *really*, *very*, and *that*. These dilute your creativity and take away from your intended final product. Readers are so accustomed to reading these common terms, they skim right over them. If you had a **really** important point to make, it might be missed using the following **very** ordinary terms:

really	that	just
very	with	then
little	so	get
big	look	was

These are only a few examples. Note the words you tend to overuse and make it a point to change them.

Do the following short exercise to see how talented you are at coming up with alternate phrases for those overused words.

WORD EXERCISE
SUBSTITUTES FOR THE OVERUSED

Provide more creative, interesting replacement sentences for the following **really** awful ones. Write more than one answer for each in your notebook, if you can.

1. I **was looking** at this **really big** caterpillar.

2. The **tiny** mouse ran past the fence to **get** food.

3. My **little** sister is the one **with** the **very** important job.

4. I **was** surprised to see you at the airport **so** I told you **that I was** supposed to **get** out of the country.

5. It **was just** a **little** cut, but it kept bleeding and bleeding.

DO THE EVENT TEST

In order to determine whether all of the happenings you included in your essay are important, try what I call **The Event Test**.

THE EVENT TEST

This test will help you to trim the actions and events included in your essay leaving only those with importance and impact.

1. **Read** through the essay, marking down a two or three word phrase in the margin to highlight each happening.

   Example:
   In the Halloween essay, the following terms highlight the events in each paragraph.
   Confidence/ wrong day/ ridicule/ heckling/ retaliation/ teacher cutting/ blue ribbon/ change clothes/ inner strength/ throughout careers/ facing obstacles/ referring back/ still growing.

2. **Examine** each phrase and ask yourself, Is this redundant?   Is it essential to understand the point of the story? Does it support the theme? Does it build off of the point before it and does it lead to the one following? If omitted, would the story remain unchanged?

3. **Omit** accordingly. If you hesitate when you ask, "Do I need this?", then you probably don't and it can go. Omit, omit, omit. This keeps the story concise, clear and easy to follow.

   Example:
   If I were to rewrite the Halloween essay now, I would omit the "throughout careers" paragraph. (See example in number 1, above.) This could be done without changing the outcome or impact of the essay.

Remember, I believe in the old saying, "The Shorter, The Better". I also support a variation of this, for new writers, "The Shorter, The Quicker to Sell. (See "The Shorter, The Better" in Chapter Four.)

JOIN A WRITER'S GROUP OR FORM ONE

One of the most valuable actions a writer can take is to network with other writers. You can attend conferences and speeches which are helpful, but the one thing you'll benefit the most from is actually meeting with writers and critiquing your own work on a regular basis.

Reading aloud to yourself can aid in finding most of the fundamental flaws in your essays, but the advantages of reading aloud to another writer or group of writers are limitless. It is **not** advisable to read to a non-writing friend or relative. He listens with a bias of love—hopefully. In other words, his opinion will **not** be objective. And while he might be able to tell you which parts are repetitive or uninteresting, the feedback you will receive from a group of writers is far more thorough and objective.

Check your local library and bookstores for a writer's group meeting there. If there aren't any, talk to librarians and store owners about recruiting writers in their announcements or newsletters. Most are supportive and are sincerely interested in promoting and helping writers.

Tell everyone you are a writer. My first group consisted of two people and was formed after a woman overheard me talking about my writing with a local librarian. She invited me to her house and we met regularly, thereafter.

I belong to several professional organizations which provide helpful information including monthly or quarterly newsletters. But the feedback I receive weekly from local writers in my critique group is invaluable.

Chapter Seven

RINSE YOUR CUP
SUBMIT

Now that the creative work is over, how do you send your story to an editor? Which editor do you choose?

FINAL MANUSCRIPT FORMAT

There are no rigid rules for how a manuscript should look, but there are some definite no-no's as far as submitting your essays. What follows is how I have chosen to present my work. You will see various formats in other publications, as every writer has her own style. But, for now, this is what works for me. Please, adhere to these guidelines in order to come across as a professional.

✓ Margins

Margins should be at least 1½″ wide—including the top, left and right. The bottom margin must be a minimum of 1″. Wide margins might look odd to you at first, but they make for a clean presentation and allow plenty of space for written comments, if an editor desires to do so.

✓ Use Typewriter-like Font

The best font choice is "Courier"—or something similar in 12 pitch—which is an option on most computers and word processors. Remember, your editor has been reading all day. The simpler fonts are easier for him to read. Fancier fonts indicate to editors you are a beginner. Professional writers use clean, simple fonts.

This is Courier, 12 pitch. See how easy it is to read with an even amount of space between each letter.

While this print looks like you have the latest computer technology—and you might hope it will impress the editor—it will only frustrate him. This is "loopy" and difficult to read.

And as far as handwritten manuscripts go, editors won't read them. If you don't have access to a typewriter or computer, you might have to pay a typist to ready your essay. You can find typists for hire in your local paper, the yellow pages, or in national writing magazines like *Writer's Digest* and *The Writer*.

✓ Double-Space

Your manuscript should *always* be double-spaced between the lines, even if you feel it is a waste of paper. Again, this is for ease of reading and a neat, clean appearance. Editors will not read single-spaced manuscripts. They are too cumbersome.

✓ Don't Use Bold or Large Print

This, too, is distracting and does not impress an editor. I will occasionally underline or italicize a word to clarify the use of that word in the sentence.

Example:

To write, "She would have called, had she had the time" has a different meaning than, "She *would* have called, had she had the time".

Hear the difference in the way the sentences are read. In a way, italicizing adds *attitude*.

BONUS TIP: When you need to emphasize a word or phrase, do so by underlining or italicizing.

✓ The First Page

In the top, left-hand corner of the first page of your manuscript, you should include your name, address, phone number, facsimile number, and e-mail address, if applicable. This information should be single-spaced. A few spaces down, include an approximate word count. This is helpful to the editor because she knows how much column space she has to fill.

Approximately halfway down the page, put the title in all capital letters, double space, then add the byline. Double space, again, indent and begin the double-spaced text. I use the Tab default on my computer which amounts to 12 spaces.

Subsequent pages of the manuscript should contain a header with your last name, a slash and a key word from your title. Some writers put their phone numbers on all pages.

✓ Page Numbering

My preference for page numbering is in the upper right-hand corner. Never number the first page.

BONUS TIP: Some references advise you to put your Social Security Number on the first page of your manuscript. The editor will need this information before she can issue you a check, if she decides to buy your essay. **I am not comfortable with giving out this personal information,** when you have not, yet, sold the piece. When you *do* sell, the editor will call and you can give her your Social Security Number over the phone or on the contract they send through the mail.

BONUS TIP: Some writing references, also, advise you to put the copyright symbol (©) at the top of the first page along with the rights you are offering. To me, this indicates that you are afraid the editor will *steal* your work. I think using the copyright symbol shouts, "amateur", and **do not recommend doing so**. Editors will assume what you are submitting is your own and is copyrighted material.

BONUS TIP: Your essay need not be registered with the Copyright Office in order to be protected, although this is possible for a small fee. The minute you record something on paper, sign your name to it and date it, it is considered yours. A simple way to protect your work is by sending a copy of the essay to yourself through the U.S. Postal Service. When you receive it back in the mail, do not open it. This sealed copy, with the date stamped on the envelope, will stand up in any court of law.

BONUS TIP: Remember, you cannot copyright an idea.

NOTE: See the sample manuscript on the following two pages.

Judith Burnett Schneider
P.O. Box 207
Ingomar, PA 15127
PHONE:(555)555-5555
FAX: (555)555-5556

Approximate word count: 175

THE MEANING OF LIFE

by

Judith Burnett Schneider

It is difficult to say exactly what the meaning of
life is. Instead of trying, then, I will type anything, here,
so you can see what your manuscript format should look like.
Isn't this clean and easy to read?

Now, it is evident why editors like this format.
They can read through the text quickly and evaluate whether
they want to send you a check or not.

Note the wide margins. This provides plenty of
space for editorial comments. Also, be sure to leave a ragged
right edge, not squared off. In other words, do not use full
justification.

If you follow these guidelines, you have given yourself a fair chance with an editor. You will not be rejected on the basis of format and you will not make the mistakes of an amateur. More than half of all manuscripts received by editors contain fundamental mistakes.

Of course, there is no guarantee of acceptance, but if you come across as a professional, you will gain the respect of the editor and other writers, immediately.

THE COVER LETTER

I could develop an entire book on the cover letter alone. Instead, I will tell you what works for me. In time, you will alter this format to best fit your individual preferences. For now, this is a safe place to start.

✓ Type

Type your cover letter, using **single spacing** between lines and **double spacing** between paragraphs.

✓ Use White Paper

Some writers think a bright pink cover letter will attract the editor's attention. It will, but in a negative light. Colored paper is unprofessional, as are colored envelopes. White, 20-pound paper or heavier is recommended.

✓ *Never* Exceed One Page

Never allow your cover letter to be longer than one page, single-spaced. You may use a different font for the cover letter than you used for the manuscript, but choose something business-like and conservative. Nothing fancy.

✓ Address to a *Specific* Editor

Use an editor's full name in the greeting of your cover letter. You can't always tell if he or she is a man or a woman, so omit Mr./Mrs. Letters not addressed to an editor by name are usually read last and end up in the slush pile. Obtain a copy of the magazine you are targeting and read the masthead to find a specific name.

BONUS TIP: Never submit to a Managing Editor. She manages people, not manuscripts. Often, I will choose a **Senior Editor** over the **Editor-in-Chief**, who probably isn't reading manuscripts either.

✓ Open With a Catchy Phrase

In your opening line, include a clever or catchy, but not cutsie, phrase. Often, writers will begin their letters with a direct quote from the work they are trying to sell. I usually open with my interpretation of the **relevance** or **timeliness** of the piece, along with a quick summarizing statement. This gives the editor reason to purchase the essay before she even reads it.   It lends the essay marketability.

Examples: Below are a few examples of opening lines from actual cover letters I have sent to editors.

✓ "Putting a new twist on the age-old question of whether to take the boss coffee or not, the enclosed essay, *The Pivotal Cup*, gives a unique answer to women."

✓ "While summer vacations should be relaxing, many people find themselves struggling through those restless nights in uncomfortable hotel beds."

✓ "Linking the approaching holidays—Mother's Day and Memorial Day—the enclosed essay, *A Mother's Memorial*, highlights a time when I came to understand my grandmother's decision **not** to bury her son in Arlington National Cemetery."

✓ This example uses an actual quote from the essay as the opening paragraph.

"'Who would cook the Thanksgiving turkey? At first, neither of us wanted the honor. My cooking expertise was limited to boxed macaroni and cheese, packaged kielbasa and, my favorite, frozen peas. I happened to be *more* qualified, though, than my husband whose gourmet talent comprised take-out in any form...'"

BONUS TIP: If you have met the editor, spoken with him on the phone, read his recent book, etc., always put that *first*—even before your clever line. Editors have egos, so if you have **a compliment or a reason to thank them**, do so in your opening. This doesn't mean you will sell, but chances are good your work will be read.

✓ Include Your Credentials

By the second paragraph—or third, if you have met the editor—list your publishing credits. If you don't have **relevant** credits, i.e. if you've published only for children and are submitting for adults, give a summary of non-relevant publishing history. Be sure to include letters to the editor, newsletters contributions or clips from other local publications, no matter how small. If you don't have any writing credits, **don't write**, "I am not published but—" And never say, "My friends or my English teacher loved this essay." The editor doesn't care. Instead, tell her you are a member of a critique group or have recently attended a conference, then give the conference name and location. This tells the editor you are serious about your writing.

Also, in this paragraph, let the editor know you have enclosed clippings of your previously published work, if applicable.

In the next paragraph, thank her for her time and consideration.

✓ Sign the Letter

This might seem like trivial advice, but I have talked with editors who say it is amazing how many letters they receive unsigned. This turns the editor off, indicating you might have submitted too quickly, without checking your enclosures before sealing the envelope.

✓ *Always* include a Self-Addressed Stamped Envelope

A self-addressed stamped envelope—commonly referred to as an SASE—must be included with each submission. Attach enough postage to return your manuscript and any letter the editor might wish to include. If you are uncertain about the postage amount and cannot have the letter weighed, add more postage than necessary. Without enough postage or with no SASE at all, you will **not** hear from the editor.

BONUS TIP: When submitting overseas or to Canadian publications, you will need to enclose a self-addressed envelope, SAE.   Instead of postage, however, you will have to purchase and enclose **International Reply Coupons** or IRC's.   The postal service will help you decide how many you will need to purchase.   Do not attach the IRC's.   Simply paper clip them to the SAE.

✓ Submit Using First-Class Mail

Use the US Postal Service and send your mail first class.   Any other way is deemed unprofessional. Do **not** send the submission certified or overnight express.   If you do so, someone must be there to sign for it and this irritates editors.   By sending first class, most manuscripts arrive at their destination within 2-3 days.

✓ FAX and Electronic Submissions

These should be saved for editors with whom you are familiar.   I discourage using alternative methods of submission for your initial contact, unless a publications specifically requests faxed or e-submissions.   For now, go the old-fashioned route via the U.S. Postal Service.   Once you establish a relationship with an editor, you can customize your submission procedure.

BONUS TIP: There are many controversial subjects in the writing community, one of which is whether to use the **multiple submissions** technique or not.   This is the practice of sending out the same manuscript to several editors at the same time. Many writers do this, but **I do not agree with the practice.**

I believe in submitting to one editor at a time. Some editors are offended by the idea that an item wasn't written specifically for her. The argument against this is that sometimes you wait weeks, even months, for a reply. I feel, if you have enough work out there—different essays on different editors desks—you won't be waiting for only one reply. You will receive mail—and possibly checks—not only monthly, but weekly.

You make the choice, but should you decide to submit to several editors at once, you must let the editor know by stating so in your cover letter.

If you do **not** choose the multiple submissions route, it is a plus to let the editor know this. For example, you could state in your closing paragraph, "This is an exclusive submission" or "This is <u>not</u> a multiple submission."

NOTE: See sample cover letter on the following page.

Judith Burnett Schneider
P.O. Box 207
Ingomar, PA 15127
PHONE: (555) 555-5555
FAX: (555) 555-5556

Date

James Smith
Editor
I Will Buy Magazine
222 Purchase Plaza
Hopeville, PA 00000

Dear James Smith:

Many thanks for taking the time to speak with me at the North Hills Writer's Conference on September 23 at the Hotel Amazia. I appreciated your advice on pacing and have successfully applied it to my writing.

Enclosed is the essay I mentioned to you. With spring around the corner, this essay, entitled SMUGGLED BULBS, might be of interest to you. It highlights a time when I witnessed the smuggling of Holland bulbs into Bulgaria and the impact of the this act on the people there. The essay is approximately 900 words in length.

My essays have appeared in *You Will Make It Magazine* and in *Pick Me Up News*, the newspaper of Successville, PA. My essay, "Home to Juneau", about my return to Alaska, placed third in the *National Writers* essay contest. I have enclosed two recent clips for your review.

Thank you for your time and consideration. I look forward to hearing from you.

Sincerely,

Judith Burnett Schneider

MARKETS

What follows are tips on how to gather new markets, choose the right one for your essay, and keep track of your submissions.

✓ Gathering Potential Markets

Everywhere you look there are potential markets for your essays. You must spend the time to find them and keep accurate records of your findings. Below is a list of ways to gather new markets. Be sure to keep all the names and addresses you've taken the time to collect in a particular place—an index card file, an envelope, your essay notebook.

✅ Keep Your Eyes Open

In order to know where to send your work, you must read and study both local and national publications. Everywhere you go—the doctor's office, the coffee shop, a friend's house—scan the magazines and newspapers. Undoubtedly, they will be different from the ones you read and might contain essays similar to the kind you write.

✅ Buy Out-of-Town Papers

If you have a friend or relative going out of town, ask them to buy a local paper or two in the city they are visiting and to grab the in-flight magazine or local interest papers as well. I recommend you do the same, whether traveling to a nearby town or across the country.

Example:
On a six-hour car trip home from South Bend, Indiana, my husband and I stopped five times, buying Sunday papers in different towns. This is how I came across the *Cleveland Plain Dealer* and found that its Sunday magazine had a personal accounts column, called *I Say*, in which my essay, "The Ears of Halloween", later appeared.

We also picked up the free tourist magazines. Sometimes those editors publish personal essays or would be willing to do so.

BONUS TIP: You can purchase out-of-town papers at the big chain bookstores and some grocery stores but the cost is sometimes quadruple the cover price.

✓ Visit the Chain Bookstores

Go to Borders, Barnes & Noble and the like. Spend time in their periodical sections where you can gather incredible amounts of information. You'll find new markets by leafing through national magazines and out-of-town newspapers. Take notes. Be sure to give yourself several hours to do this. It can be quite time-consuming.

Remember, while doing so, to jot down addresses and editors' names and titles. Then, go home and write a priority list of where your essay should be sent first, second, third, etc., based on the style and content of the essays the different publications printed.

✓ Check *Writer's Market*

This book is an essential tool in researching national markets and regional markets in other areas. It is an annual publication by Writer's Digest Books which includes a nearly-comprehensive list of markets, what they publish, what they pay, response times, addresses, phone numbers and editors' names. (See *Recommended Reading*.)

✓ Clandestine Markets

The most viable markets for you might be those **not** listed in *Writer's Market*. These editors are not likely to receive as large a volume of submissions as those listed in the international publication. Because submissions are fewer—and you have taken the time and effort to write your essay effectively and present your work professionally—it is in these clandestine markets where you will have the most luck, initially.

How do you find these clandestine markets? As I stated earlier, you discover these high-potential markets by keeping your eyes open for interesting, new, even esoteric, publications wherever you go.

✓ Zeroing In

✓ Study.

It is of utmost importance to study the magazine or newspaper to which you intend to submit. Read two or more recent issues and try to assess the style and content of essays that editor publishes. Then, decide whether your work would be suitable for that market. This way, you will not waste your time—or the editor's—by submitting to a publication which doesn't print essays or doesn't use those of the style or content of your manuscript.

This sounds like trivial advice but, again, editors have told me how numerous their *irrelevant* submissions are.

Example:

Do not send an essay about your perspective on political corruption in lawyers practicing in the District of Columbia to a Midwestern mother's publication. It is not likely to fit their needs, thus, wasting your time and hurting your chances for publication with that editor in the future.

When you complete an essay, you'll feel anxious to get it in the mail. But if you don't do your marketing homework, you will be assured a rejection.

BONUS TIP: Research the market, first. Then, submit.

CONTESTS

An easy way to pressure yourself to submit, if that's the motivation you need, is to enter contests. You can find out about various contests at conferences and in national magazines, like *Writer's Digest* and *The Writer*, among others. These publications, and more, are available for purchase at the big chain bookstores or by subscription.

The rules provided for any contest serve as guidelines outlining exactly what is needed to qualify i.e. word count, topic, etc. And, the good thing is, there is **always a deadline**. This keeps you motivated and on track. In a way, it forces you to submit.

BONUS TIP: Often, contests require you to include a reading fee with your entries. This is acceptable and legitimate. However, I would not recommend you enter contests requesting over $20 per manuscript.

BOOKKEEPING

Selling your writing is a business and, like any other small business, you must keep accurate records. I have designed two essential charts for organizing your writing business: **The Submission Record** and **The Expense Record.** A sample of each is included at the end of this section.

It is important to keep accurate records of where you have submitted which particular essays and what type of response you received. This seems simple now, but once you've written 12 essays, for example, and they are all out to different editors, the whole process can become confusing. A sure way to alienate an editor is to re-send her something she has already rejected.

You might, also, want to keep a file for each essay, stating where submitted, responses, sales, etc. A sister file to this one would list each publication, which essays were submitted there, which were purchased, amount paid, when published, etc.

You must also have on record how much money is coming in and going out. Include, on your Expense Record, books you have purchased, babysitting fees, and mileage to meetings, as well as conference fees and membership dues. You can easily offset your writing income with legitimate writing expenses. And this, of course, benefits you come April 15. Don't forget to save all receipts.

You don't have to be an accountant to keep track of these things. Each time you submit an essay or buy something related to your writing, jot it down on a chart like the ones I have included here.

BONUS TIP: When you receive a check from the sale of an essay, record it as income on your Expense Record.

Keeping track of your submissions and expenses is the key to running your freelance writing business both accurately and efficiently.

SUBMISSIONS

#	DATE	SENT TO	RESPONSE DATE	COMMENTS	WHERE TO SEND NEXT
1	May 18	The Daily Gazette	May 30	Accepted/wants to see more of my work.	Try to re-sell to *Reader's Digest*.
2					
3					
4					
5					
6					

EXPENSES

DATE	DESCRIPTION	AMOUNT	FORM*	(INCOME)
May 12	*Write Well & Sell* Book		Check #1272	
May 30	Sold Essay to Daily Gazette.			($75.00)

*Include method of payment: Check, Cash, or Charge.

Chapter Eight

RELAX BETWEEN CUPS
WAIT FOR A RESPONSE

HOW LONG TO WAIT

For submissions to newspapers, you should hear from the editor, either by phone or by mail, within two months. For magazines, you might have to wait anywhere from two weeks to six months. My advice is to wait no longer than **two months**. This gives the publication plenty of time to look over your work and respond. After two months, it is time to take action.

WHEN TO CALL

Many writers will tell you it is a big no-no to call editors. They are busy and need to spend their time sorting through submissions, attending meetings, etc. To that I quote my four-year-old by saying, "Fooey".

My submission is important and if they can't review it and respond in two month's time, I want it back.

BONUS TIP: If you are not comfortable on the phone, you might want to contact the editor in

writing. Be sure to state the title of your essay and when it was submitted. Don't forget to include another SASE.

There are strict guidelines on when to call an editor. I recommend you contact her about two months after your submission date, if you have not heard. Allow an additional two weeks or so if it is the summer or around the holidays. Editors take vacations, too.

Examples:

Remember to be polite and keep it short. The conversation should go something like this:

ME: "Hello, Mr. Jones. My name is Judith Burnett Schneider. I submitted an essay to you on February 1 of this year, called "The Pivotal Cup", about refusing to take your boss coffee. I was interested in checking the status of the submission."

He will respond in one of several ways.

✓ **EDITOR**: "I seem to recall the essay, but we are not interested in publishing it. You should be receiving it back soon."

ME: "Thank you for your consideration. I hope to send you something else soon."

✓ **EDITOR**: "I don't recall receiving the submission. Would you mind sending it again?"

ME: "Not at all. But can I write something, in particular, on the envelope to insure it will reach you."

EDITOR: "Yes. Write 'Requested Material' (or whatever).

ME: "Thank you for your time. I'll get that to you by next week."

✓ **EDITOR**: "I enjoyed your essay very much and sent it to Final Review upstairs. They should be making a decision within the next four weeks."

ME: "Thank you for your time. I'll wait to hear from you."   Then, I hang up the phone, hoot, and jump around the study.

Notice, I didn't say, "Hey, why didn't you like my work?" or "What didn't you like about the essay?" This is childish and unprofessional.

BONUS TIP: Never call an editor to ask, "What are you looking for?" Her standard answer will be something like, "Good writing."

The truth is, editors don't mind calls from professionals who keep to the point, find out what they need and hang up. They do mind calls from pesky writers who want to complain or ask inappropriate questions.

BONUS TIP: Never call an editor to tell her about the great idea you have. Professional writers submit *manuscripts* not *ideas*. Also, if you receive a rejection in the mail, **never call** to find out why the editor didn't like your work. You are an adult and must accept that not everyone will love what you write. Record it on your Submissions Record and send it out again. There is no place for hurt feelings in this business.

The way to get published is to write well, submit, and submit again. Calling editors to sell an idea or to seek editorial advice will only alienate you from them and from potential sales.

Chapter Nine

HAVE ANOTHER CUP
WRITE, AGAIN

WRITE, WRITE, WRITE

In order to succeed in the business of writing, you must write, write, write. Everyday, you should **make** time to ponder ideas, write rough drafts, or edit existing ones. At the very least, you should take the time to read newspapers or magazines, scanning for new markets and allowing current events to spark ideas.

Writing is addictive. If you stay away from it for too long, you won't *need* to write. But as you begin to create regularly, the desire to do so will gnaw at you. You won't feel satisfied until you've had your daily dose of the stuff. You will actually begin to *crave* the act of writing.

RE-SELL YOUR WORK

There is something appealing to an editor about an essay another editor thought enough of to purchase. So, if you do sell an essay, don't forget about it. Once it has been published, send it out to other markets, but be sure to tell them it has been published before. Tell them **where** and **when** and include a photocopy of the published work. You will be selling it as a reprint which sometimes pays less, sometimes not.

Example:

I, once, re-sold an essay and earned 4.5 times the amount I made on the original sale.

WRITE FOR MONEY

I advise writers to write for money. As a rule, don't write for free. In starting out, you might find yourself writing for editorial or opinion pages just to see your name in print and obtain clippings. That's fine, but as you grow in your writing, always ask for some kind of payment, be it $20.00. This separates you, the professional writer, from the wanna-be's.

NETWORKING

I can't emphasize enough the importance of networking—joining or forming a writer's group, either live or through the Internet, attending conferences, talking about writing to librarians and professionals. This is how you establish invaluable contacts and open new doors for yourself. You never know who might be listening.

It has been cleverly stated that everyone knows someone who knows someone in the world of publishing. But often, the only way to reveal this information is by continually using your resources to network.

OTHER OUTLETS

Short, personal writing can be sold in other markets including greeting cards, how-to articles, children's poems, travel pieces and fillers for magazines.

A colleague of mine, Sandra M. Louden, teaches a greeting card writing course at the local community college. I signed up—not with the intention of trying to sell greeting cards—but mostly because she was a friend and an experienced freelance writer. As it turned out, I sold my first greeting card to Oatmeal Studios just two weeks after I completed the course. That was in 1994 and I have been selling greeting card captions ever since. Sandra is the author of another book in **The Blueprint Series**, entitled *Write Well & Sell: Greeting Cards.*

In addition to greeting cards, I have sold children's poetry to *Babybug Magazine*, of *The Cricket Magazine Group*, and to *Turtle Magazine for Preschool Kids*, a publication of *The Children's Better Health Institute*.

Mary Jo Rulnick, another colleague and friend, sells short, personal writing in the form of short tip lists and everyday-advice articles. Reading the front cover of any magazine demonstrates how "in-demand" these types of articles are. For example: "Five Ways to Live on a Budget" or "15 Tips for Selling Your Home", etc.

Mary Jo is a talented individual who, with many years of experience, has written another book in this series, called *Write Well & Sell: How-To Articles.* She is one of the best "advice-givers" I know. In writing, and in life, her tips on organizing, using time wisely, and turning your interests into cash are *always* usable and doable.

NOTES:

The Ears of Halloween

An Essay by Judith Burnett Schneider

I don't know if it surfaced on that memorable Halloween eve, but it was the first time I recalled feeling confidence, strength of character, the power of free will.

As I approached the massive double doors, an inner voice, which had never so much as whispered, shouted, "Don't wear the bunny ears." I didn't, though my body was prisoner to the grey flannel bunny suit.

Filling my lungs, I gripped the door handle. What if my mother were right? No. I was sure the Halloween Parade was today, October 30th. I exhaled, swinging the heavy door out of my way. Forty-eight kindergarten eyes and two authoritative ones froze on the figure, a grey flannel bunny minus ears—me. For a second, thoughts of stardom flashed across my mental screen. Reality followed. My bunny costume was neither fantastic, nor a flop. It was simply misplaced, out of context.

The 48 eyes belonged to my classmates who weren't in costume, students who didn't dress up on the wrong day. Laughter and ridicule ensued. The grey bunny statue stood gripping a green duffel bag, framed by the double doors of room 10. After an immobile moment, I smiled, straightened my stance, and pranced toward my seat.

Frederick heckled, "Wrong day, dumb bunny."

"Goofy Judy," Alexander yelled. Even Anna, my best friend, as friends go at age five, covered her mouth and pointed. The teacher attempted to maintain order, although surely in her 30 years of teaching, she had never seen this. No pupil had ever worn a costume on the day *before* Halloween.

I spun in front of my seat, spread my arms and dropped the duffle bag. Instead of being tongue-tied, I was articulate. I addressed my current classmates and former friends. "Tomorrow, all of you will be dressed-up together. Today, I'll win the blue ribbon for best costume."

Mrs. Stewart backed me up, as any good, and momentarily desperate, kindergarten teacher would. "That's right, Judy," she said, fishing through the top drawer of her desk. She carried a piece of blue construction paper and a pair of scissors. She was the ultimate cutter and her hands were fast at work.

I accepted my imitation blue ribbon with pride and was startled by the applause initiated by Alexander. I even heard Frederick say, "Great idea to dress-up early. I wish I had thought of it."

Despite my merited blue ribbon, I quickly changed into the clothes my intuitive mother packed for me in the green duffle bag. The rest of the afternoon was a blur.

Overall, that memorable Halloween was a good one, however challenging. Humiliated, I could have been. Embarrassed, I should have been. Instead, I forced myself to feel a sense of individuality, of accomplishment. I was in costume on the wrong day, there was no hiding that. But I was unique and I was strong.

Many times since the Great Halloween Mistake, I have called upon the strength and determination uncovered that day. I've relied on the spirit of that moment throughout my years as a student of science, and during my careers as a research chemist and writer, thereafter. I was discouraged, and plowed ahead. I was disheartened, and stood forthright. I wanted to be, and I became.

Recently, another writer commented that I should know what it was like to fight against the odds as a woman in the male-dominated field of science. Truthfully, I didn't. Or at least I didn't realize it. I never saw myself as a woman in a lab coat, although as a pregnant woman in a lab coat, my gender was difficult to deny. I was a scientist who happened to be a woman. I didn't want to land any job or achieve any goal because I fulfilled some government-instituted quota. I wanted to be chosen because I was the best suited for the job, the candidate who could *deliver*.

I am who I am today because it is who I wanted to be. For others, Christmas and Thanksgiving induce reflection and introspection. My holiday is Halloween. Each October thirtieth, I reminisce. I wear the grey flannel suit *and* the ears. I admire the courage of a five-year-old who found a way, who dared to stand out. I revere the moment I gained by losing.

Although I don't dress-up on the wrong day anymore, I still make mistakes. And I strive to learn something new from each of them. Even now, I enjoy dressing in costume on Halloween night.   And although I might masquerade as a witch, a ghost, or an angel with wings, there was only one Halloween for the bunny without ears.

This essay originally appeared in *The Pittsburgh Tribune-Review*, then in *The Cleveland Plain Dealer*.

The Saint Valentine's Day Sleighing
An Essay by Judith Burnett Schneider

This essay effectively uses the recommendations from The Trick List in Chapter Five and The Don'ts List in Chapter Six. Read it carefully, looking for use of alliteration, theme, the magical rule of three, etc.

From behind the wheel of my compact import, it was difficult to decipher where my husband and I were supposed to be. Visibility was about fourteen inches and our only boundaries were the three-foot snow banks along each side of what was probably the road. Despite the flurries predicted in the city and ten inches in the mountains, I decided not to abandon my original plan to surprise my husband on an otherwise ordinary February 14th. Judging from the pressure behind my swelled ear drums and the height of the drifted snow, we were undoubtedly in the mountains and optimistically more than halfway there—halfway to our hopefully romantic destination.

Without checking the dashboard digital, my stomach told me that we wouldn't be making our six o'clock dinner reservation at the secluded country inn. Perhaps I should have chosen a romantic evening closer to home, like take-out Asian cuisine or white pizza from the corner shop. Then again, I didn't want white-anything after an hour of fighting the nations greatest snow storm.

"Dear," I said—we were near-newlyweds then—"I need food." Though I spoke softly, my husband knew from experience this meant, "GET ME FOOD NOW, OR I'LL LOSE CONSCIOUSNESS."

He motioned for me to pull to the side of the road.

"Good thing I brought the usual Survival Kit," I said, looking for a pat on the back.

"Good thing," he said sarcastically, patting my back. It was ritual for him to reluctantly load the trunk with a large yellow bag full of everything one might need in a snow-related emergency, including two full length ski suits, knee high double insulated boots, down-stuffed leather mittens, fully lined ski hats, Scottish wool scarves, a shovel, and **food**—two boxes of crackers and a six-pack of mountain spring water. It wasn't Brie and chardonnay but it sure beat tree bark and melted snow. This would be the first time we used any of the yellow bag's contents, even if it were just the food.

Waiting for a level stretch of road, I slowed to a stop in the right side of our lane—the shoulder no longer evident—and waited as my husband went to retrieve the Survival Kit. Through the windshield, I spotted the only non-white part of our snow-covered surroundings. Approximately eleven feet in front of the car was a fresh sample of road kill. My thoughts turned to my sister who, at thirty, calls the unsightly blobs "dead kill" as if there were some other kind like "lingering kill" or "comatose kill". Suddenly, the back door opened. Snow and wind cut through the car's cavity. The entire vehicle began to rock as my husband forced the four-feet wide yellow Survival Kit through the two-and-a-half foot opening allowed by the import's back door.

While plowing half-speed ahead, we munched

bland biscuits, sipped spring water, and talked about world politics, office management, and our niece's new eye tooth—a discussion which included why it's called an "eye tooth" and not something more appealing like "optic tooth" or "visual organ tooth". Romantic? So far so good.

Finally, a red and white sign revealed what had remained a secret throughout our perilous journey. Surprise. This Valentine's Day, we were going a-sleighing.

I shivered with delight despite the warmth of the cozy mountain lodge. Upon completing the necessary check-in and check-signing, we were escorted to the sleighing sight. This would be our first sleigh ride together, alone. At least I hoped we'd be alone. In my haste to plan an unforgettably romantic evening, did I neglect to reserve the entire sleigh for ourselves? After enduring hours behind the wheel, fighting snow, road kill, and hunger, would we be sleighing over mountaintops with chatty strangers, a preschool class of thirty or, worse yet, ten teens who might label us as, heaven forbid, *old*?

Fortunately, we were the only ones scheduled for the 8:00 sleigh ride. Unfortunately, we were escorted to a sixteen-year-old brown station wagon with matching wood-grained panels, a roof rack, and snow-chains covering each tire. We exchanged looks of concern, mine saying "This is odd" and his saying "What kind of sleigh did you rent?". We sat in the back seat of the Dilapidated Taxi, hands clutched in silence. Romantic? Not quite.

Noticing the three-inch thick ice, layered with

frozen mud and rock, I instinctively reached for my seat belt. It had either been sucked forever into the bowels of the vehicle or purposely removed. My head jerked as we began our seemingly interminable sideways spinning skid up the treacherous mountainside path. Eventually, despite my furrowed brows, squeezed-shut eyelids, and translucent knuckles, I sensed level ground. Then, a storybook clearing and a waiting horse-drawn sleigh. It had already been worth the trip.

The untouched snow sparkled under the strategically placed spotlights. Floundering flakes danced, as if only for us, finally resting in a decorative layer over the plaid wool blanket that protected us from the crisp winter wind. As we floated along, I took in the breathtaking scene. The land stretched out before us like shimmering meadows of marshmallow cream dotted with chocolate sticks and an occasional gingerbread barn. The ride lasted forty-five minutes. The experience was the closest to "fairy tale" we had ever come—soft music piped in from who-knows where, a now crystal clear, star-speckled sky, and the warmth of my Valentine.

As the sleigh glided to a halt, something caught my eye through the trees. It wasn't a lantern or a shooting star. It was a jolt back to reality—the taillight of the Dilapidated Taxi—*our only way down*.

We assumed crash positions in the vehicle, swerving, skidding, and somehow dodging large trees and small animals.

My husband and I were chilled and worn,

needing a source of warmth and relaxation. Once safely in front of the lodge fire tasting appetizers and fine wine, I realized our Valentine's Day celebration was drawing to a close. We had weathered the weather, were taxed by the taxi, and toured the countryside in a horse-drawn sleigh. Was the evening exhilarating and fulfilling? Was it memorable and unique? It was all that and more. The Valentine surprise was worth it all.

And was it romantic? You bet.

This essay originally appeared in *The Pittsburgh Tribune-Review*.

THE AFTERTASTE

The two most important things I hope to leave you with are motivation and direction. Just a few years ago, I was where you are—reading everything I could get my hands on about how to improve my writing, how to submit and how to earn.

Now that you have completed reading this book, the next step is to write. You have learned what you need to know, so give the process an honest try. Take a unique idea, write a first draft, add in a few of the tricks I recommended, edit out the excess and submit. I urge you to do this, **now**. I spent too much time, when I started out, trying to perfect my writing and stalling my efforts to send work to editors. After you have learned to recognize flaws in your writing and have changed them according to my simple tips, you are ready. Don't waste time, like I did.

Submit. And learn from your submissions. Note which editors respond to your work and which publications accept work similar to yours. Experience what it feels like to receive a check in the mail and see your name in print.

I invite you to contact me with questions or comments. If you feel this book helped you write higher quality essays and sell them, please let me know. Please inform me, too, if there is some topic you would like to see covered in future editions of this book or in the series, in general.

Address all correspondence to me at the following address:

P.O. Box 207
Ingomar, PA 15127

Please enclose a self-addressed stamped envelope if you would like a response. You may also e-mail me at:

jbswrites@sgi.net

If you would like to order additional copies of this book, or order others in the series, write:

Jam-Packed Press
P.O. Box 9701
Pittsburgh, PA 15229

As you look in newspapers and magazines, you will see many of the rules I covered in this text being neglected or broken by other writers. And now that you know what you know, you will find many poorly written essays in print. This should not be a discouraging, but a motivational, finding.

Don't hesitate. Enter the writing world, **now**, by writing well and submitting to sell. Prove to editors tomorrow that you are better than the writers they are publishing today.

Many Thanks and Good Luck!

Recommended Reading

While you ponder your essay idea and order your thoughts, you might want to read any or all of the following recommendations:

Gerard, Philip, editor. *Creative Nonfiction.*
This term refers to an approach to nonfiction which involves the reporting of facts presented in a story or fictional format from an actual perspective i.e. often told through the point of view of the writer instead of as cold narrative.

An excellent creative nonfiction example is a book by Joyce Dyer about her mother's battle with Alzheimer's Disease, entitled *In a Tangled Wood: An Alzheimer's Journey.*

A second recommended example of creative nonfiction is the best-seller, *Midnight in the Garden of Good and Evil* by John Berendt. This is an account of a murder investigation in Savannah including a cast of unique characters. This book is completely factual, yet reads like fiction.

NOTE: I like to define the books in this growing genre as *extremely* long essays.

Hodges, John C. and Whitten, Mary E. *Harbrace College Handbook.*

This invaluable reference is packed with information on proper usage of punctuation, grammar, sentence structure, and paragraph format. It might not be on the shelves in your local bookstore, but it can be ordered. The book is easy to use with an index that allows you to find what you need within seconds. It includes common mistakes made in grammar, etc. including ones you might not have realized were incorrect. It is extremely accurate, specific and useful.

Lamott, Anne. *bird by bird.*

This book highlights insights into the philosophy of writing and the writing life. It is loaded with quotable, memorable, well-crafted segments with which any true writer can readily identify.

Simon, Rachel. *The Writer's Survival Guide.*

I was privileged to hear Rachel Simon speak at a conference. Like her, this book is insightful and informative. She holds nothing back in instructing on how to write and revise fiction. I believe her techniques to hold true for essays, as well, and that reading this would be worth your while. Simon, also, addresses the philosophy of writing and the "psyche" of the writer. This is an excellent, easy read.

Spooner, Alan compiled. *Oxford Minireference Thesaurus.*
Liebeck, Helen and Pollard, Elaine, editors. *Oxford English Minidictionary.*

These were a gift from my husband and, while he has given me more exclusive gifts, I was delighted to receive them. They are extremely convenient, because of their size, and easy to flip through, due to their soft covers. While reading and writing, I can quickly look up the words I need. These books put the potential for an "expanded vocabulary", literally at your fingertips.

Strunk, Jr., William and White, E. B. *The Elements of Style.*

No matter your style or voice, every writer must have a copy of this book close at hand, even if you think you have an incredible handle on the English language. It is essential to know where to put a semi-colon or when to use the subjunctive. Nothing turns an editor off more—as long as you've spelled her name correctly—than fundamental mistakes in grammar and spelling. Always check your work and use this as a guide.

Writer's Digest Books. *Writer's Market.*

This book is a great overview and unmistakably the most comprehensive listing of writing markets available. I was given this as a gift when I began my professional writing career, and what a boost. It sends you in the right direction, right away.   In addition to names, addresses and phone numbers of newspapers, magazines, and book publishers, *Writer's Market* tells how much each pays and includes their response time.   It also highlights one-page interviews of prominent people in various fields with legitimate advice on writing technique and manuscript format. I can't say enough about this publication.